JAPANESE STYLE
PLANT-BASED COOKING

Amazing Vegan Recipes from Japan's
Leading Macrobiotic Chef and Food Writer

Yumiko Kano

TUTTLE Publishing

Tokyo │ Rutland, Vermont │ Singapore

Contents

Making the Most of Your Vegetables

PICKLING:
Preserved Goodness

Vegetables and Me

"My journey as a vegetarian chef is truly a history of overcoming my dislike of vegetables!"

I started cooking around the time I began elementary school because I didn't like the vegetable dishes my mother cooked. I wanted something tastier, so I started reading cookbooks.

Later, when I left home to start college, my parents, who were farmers, would send me lots of vegetables and it was a struggle to use them all. I developed an interest in trying to make full-course feasts using vegetables only.

Among the cookbooks I'd been reading since I was a child, I could never find one that suited my tastes. Over time I began to accumulate my own recipes, and become more confident with ingredients and seasonings.

In the search for ideal vegetable dishes, the scope of my activities expanded. My sister and I opened a store selling vegetable buns. Around the same time, I started catering dinner parties, offering vegetable-only courses. I have been involved with a sustainability-themed hotel in Nepal, and I opened a vegetarian restaurant in Japan. I also organized vegetarian cooking classes and vegetarian cooking tours abroad.

One thing I noticed was that there are few dishes in Japanese cuisine that make the most of vegetables. Because Japan is surrounded by the sea and has a long

TOP LEFT: I grow my own organic vegetables at home in rural Tottori Prefecture, using organic fertilizers and no chemicals.
LEFT: On a visit to the country of Georgia, I made vegetarian khinkali dumplings with the locals.

"I was born into a farming family, but I hated vegetables." How did Yumiko Kano's unique vegetable dishes come about?

tradition of delicious seafood, many dishes are based on seafood stock. But on my travels to other countries I found many dishes that are completely centered on vegetables. I realized that the "cuisine that brings out the best in vegetables" that I was seeking already existed in the world, and that my direction was not mistaken, which gave me confidence. Through these experiences, I have rediscovered the richness of Japanese vegetable ingredients and deepened my understanding of traditional cuisines from around the world.

Now, based in Japan's Tottori Prefecture, I travel back and forth to Tokyo, holding vegetarian cooking classes in both places and sharing vegetable recipes. In Tottori, I grow my own organic vegetables. When I think about it, vegetables have always been an important part of my life.

TOP: I share my love of vegetable cuisine with others through regular cooking classes that I hold In various locations in Japan. **TOP RIGHT:** At a supermarket in Lebanon I saw an abundance of vegetables, displayed so beautifully!
RIGHT: My younger sister and I opened a store selling vegetable buns. We gained quite a reputation, and there were huge lines and a lot of buzz.

Vegetables Can Be the Stars of the Meal!

The stars of the recipes that I will introduce in this book are vegetables. Just like meat, fish or eggs, vegetables are quite capable of playing the main role in a dish. It's just that in many cases their full potential is not brought out and they are simply left to play supporting parts.

I was born and raised in a farming family in Japan's rural Tottori Prefecture, and as a child I hated vegetables. I couldn't eat the monotonous boiled or stewed vegetable dishes that were served up every day, but because we were farmers we had more vegetables than we could eat. It was this environment that propelled me toward making my own vegetable dishes, and this was the first step on my journey to becoming a vegetarian chef.

Maybe you grow your own vegetables and have bumper crops you don't know what to do with. Or maybe you're bored with the same old vegetables you see every day in the store, and the same old cooking methods. Maybe you've just bought too many vegetables because it was cheaper to buy in bulk and now you don't know how you're going to finish them.

But what if these vegetables could be made into star-of-the-show main courses, or mouthwatering starters, or tasty snacks to enjoy with drinks? I hope this book will help you look at vegetables in a whole new way.

Maximize the Flavor of Your Vegetables

Seasonal vegetables are delicious, powerful, and full of nutrients. It is such a waste to serve such vegetables as "garnishes" with meat and fish. I hope that this book will help you discover how to enjoy eating seasonal vegetables without getting tired of them.

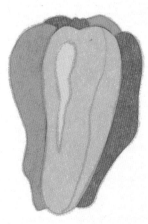

To make vegetables the star of a dish, you need to bring out the best in them. Should they be boiled, baked or sautéed? Are they cooked whole or chopped? The same vegetable can have a variety of flavors depending on how it is prepared, how it is cut, and on the seasonings used.

All recipes you will find in this book have the following three points in common:

❶ Bitterness is not removed

The bitterness and off-flavors of vegetables are not unpleasant like those of meat or fish, and they also contain umami. The recipes in this book do not attempt to get rid of bitterness—instead they use the bitterness to enhance the flavor of a dish.

❷ The vegetables are eaten with their skins on

The skin of a vegetable is full of flavor, so the recipes in this book avoid peeling as much as possible. If you can get into the habit of not peeling, you'll benefit from enhanced taste and goodness.

❸ No animal products are used

In order to bring out the gentle natural taste of vegetables, the recipes in this book do not use any animal products. Surrounded by the sea, Japan has many culinary techniques that utilize the umami of fish, including the widespread use of dashi stock made with bonito flakes, for example. However, the gentle flavors of vegetables cannot compete with the intense tastes of meat and fish, and are often overshadowed by them. If you decide to make vegetables the stars of the meal, you don't need meat or fish products.

Seasonings

The Nine Best Seasonings for Vegetables

Careful use of seasonings will maximize the natural flavor of vegetables. Use the best quality ones you can find, and experiment with new seasonings for familiar dishes.

❶ Salt

Salt is the most important seasoning for bringing out the umami and flavor of vegetables. It reduces harsh or off-putting vegetable flavors, and fixes the color for a bright finish to a dish.

Steam-simmering or steam-frying with salt is the best way to bring out the umami of vegetables. To reduce harsh flavors, blanch or boil vegetables in salted water, or stir-fry them while adding salt a little at a time. To stop the color of vegetables from leeching out, boil them briefly in water with plenty of salt added or rub them with salt before cooking.

I like sea salt with vegetables—it has a good balance of minerals and is tastier than rock salt. Whatever salt you use, make sure it is unrefined, for maximum nutrients and minerals.

❷ Soy Sauce

Fermented soybean products such as soy sauce go well with vegetables. Soy sauce has a strong umami that livens up any vegetable. Just a little will bring out the sweetness of the vegetable and reduce any harsh or bitter tastes.

I recommend products made with whole soybeans (not defatted soybeans) that have been fermented and brewed slowly using traditional methods. I also choose products with no artificial amino acids added. I believe that natural soy sauce brings out the flavor of the vegetables best.

❸ Miso

There is rice miso, wheat miso, and bean miso, depending on the type of base ingredients, and red miso and white miso, depending on the fermentation process and maturation period. Choose a long-aged product that has been cured the old-fashioned way, using mold-inoculated rice and salt. Like soy sauce, miso adds umami and richness to vegetables.

The recipes in this book use rice miso, but feel free to experiment with different types depending on your preferences or on what is easily available.

❹ Oil

For the best quality and flavor, choose products made by traditional pressing methods rather than by chemical refining.

I use canola oil as the basic cooking oil for the recipes in this book as it is lower in saturated fat than vegetable oil.

When using olive oil, I recommend aromatic extra virgin olive oil.

Sesame oil comes in light or dark varieties and you can use either for the recipes in this book, or even blend the two types together to make the most of the best features of both.

❺ Mirin

Mirin is a type of cooking wine made of rice that is a common ingredient in Japanese cuisine. It adds a deep sweetness, umami and richness to food, as well as a mellow flavor. It also adds shine and luster.

Mirin is made in a variety of ways, and chemically brewed mirin-style seasoning is widely available. I recommend "hon mirin," which is made using only mochi rice, rice malt and shochu distilled liquor.

❻ Vinegar

Recipes that call for vinegar in this book use pure rice vinegar, which is mild and well rounded in flavor.

Rice vinegar brewed by the static fermentation method, in which fermentation is naturally circulated, is recommended, rather than the fast fermentation method in which fermentation is accelerated mechanically. The former type of vinegar contains not only acidity but also umami from the rice malt, which goes well with vegetables.

Different types of vinegar can add interest to familiar dishes. Try black vinegar for umami and richness in Chinese cuisine; wine vinegar or apple cider vinegar for a fruity, fresh flavor; and balsamic vinegar for sweetness.

❼ Sake

Sake helps to reduce any tartness or harshness in a vegetable and adds flavor, umami and a hint of sweetness. It also gives cooked vegetables a nice, juicy finish.

Cooking sake is widely available but I suggest you use pure rice drinking sake for the recipes in this book that call for sake as an ingredient. Pure rice sake is brewed only with rice and rice koji, and has no added salt.

❽ Sugar

I try not to use sugar, because I want to preserve the natural sweetness of the vegetables. If I do need extra sweetness, I use beet sugar, raw cane sugar or brown sugar rather than refined white sugar. I sometimes use maple syrup or amazake (sweet sake; see this page) as sweeteners.

❻ Amazake

Amazake, which means "sweet sake," is a thick, fermented, naturally sweet low-alcohol sake used for drinking, cooking and preserving. It is often used in place of sugar and also as an ingredient in pickling beds. Some types are a little thin for use as a seasoning, so choose a condensed type that can be diluted 2 to 3 times. I also recommend making your own (see below).

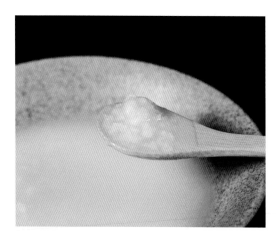

Homemade Amazake

AN EASY-TO-MAKE AMOUNT

¾ cup (150 g) mochi rice
2½ cups (600 ml) water
7 oz (200 g) dried rice koji

❶ Soak the mochi rice in the water for 2 hours, then cook in a rice cooker (see note below) to make very soft rice. Cool the rice down to 150°F (65°C).
❷ Put the rice koji in a plastic bag. Press the bag with your hands to crumble the koji grains apart.
❸ Add the rice koji to the cooked rice from Step 1 and mix well. Heat the mixture in a rice cooker or yogurt maker set to 140°F (60°C) for about 8 hours until creamy and sweet.

> **TIP:** If you don't have a rice cooker, cook the mochi rice until it is very soft, and place the hot rice in a thermal soup jar or a yogurt maker with the crumbled rice koji for at least 8 hours, until the mixture is creamy and sweet.

Preparation Methods

Eight Preparation Methods with Keys for Creating Delicious Flavor
In order to bring out the best flavor from vegetables, it is important to choose the preparation method that best suits the characteristics of the vegetable. The guide on these pages will help you.

❶ Simmering or stewing

Simmering or stewing vegetables in water or stock and seasonings will give a soft and fluffy texture and tenderness to vegetables. Gently applying heat creates a rich, sweet flavor, which is enhanced by the seasonings. The broth produced during the cooking process can be eaten with the vegetables or used as part of a soup or stew.

Take care not to overcook the vegetables. That will spoil the taste and texture.

❷ Cooking with high heat (baking, roasting, grilling)

Heating vegetables to a high temperature by baking, roasting or grilling can bring out a variety of delicious flavors, that are sharper and more distinctive than the flavors produced by stewing.

Cooking at high heat is also an effective way of eliminating unpleasant smells and tastes from many ingredients. In the case of vegetables, the longer they are cooked at high heat, the more they benefit from this effect.

❸ Stir-frying or sautéing

This cooking method is used to cook ingredients quickly, but in the case of vegetable dishes, stir-frying them a little longer brings out their sweetness and umami. If you stop cooking the vegetables too soon, you will not maximize their natural flavor, and you may be tempted to add artificial flavor enhancers.

When stir-frying vegetables use medium-high heat (rather than high heat) and move the ingredients around a little while cooking. Keep stir-frying until any excess moisture released by the vegetables during the cooking process has evaporated. Adding a little salt with help with this process and also concentrate the umami.

❹ Deep-frying

Deep-frying at a constant high temperature removes bitterness and any unpleasant odors from food, making it more palatable and bringing out the umami.

When it comes to vegetables, frying is suitable for root and fruiting types, as well as leafy greens or wild vegetables with strong aroma and taste.

❹ Boiling

Boiling is an effective way to reduce the bulk of leafy greens, but the umami of the vegetables is lost. It's a cooking method I prefer to keep to a minimum, using occasionally to prepare leafy vegetables such as spinach or komatsuna greens.

❺ Dressing or mixing

By dressing or mixing raw or cooked vegetables with different seasonings, complex tastes can be created. The varieties of dishes that can be created this way are endless, depending on the vegetable, the way the vegetables are cut, and the combination of seasonings.

❻ Drying

This is a preparation method in which ingredients are exposed to sunlight and wind to remove moisture. If dried thoroughly in this way, the food can be preserved for a long time.

If long-term preservation is not your goal, I recommend "quick drying": drying vegetables in the sun for 4–5 hours after cutting them. This not only concentrates the sweetness and umami, but it also prevents water from being released from the food, making it easier to cook and shortening the cooking time.

With the "quick drying" method, the vegetables should be dried just long enough to become slightly wilted. The longer the drying time, the longer the vegetables will keep.

❼ Steam-stewing, steam-frying

This method is a kind of "waterless cooking." The vegetables, seasonings, and on occasion a small amount of water are placed in a sealed pot and heated while steaming. This concentrates the flavor of the vegetables and brings out their umami and sweetness.

Steam-stewing means the ingredients are stewed in their own juices rather than adding water or stock. Using less liquid helps the vegetables retain their flavor. Steam-frying means the ingredients are seared or pan-fried first to seal in their juices, then steamed in their own juices or with a small amount of water added to the pan with the lid on. This method results in more succulent vegetables than simply pan-frying. A small amount of salt added at the beginning of either cooking method helps the flavors become more concentrated. For either cooking method, I recommend enameled cast-iron pots and pans that conduct and store heat well.

How to Make Kombu Dashi Stock

You can buy kombu dashi stock powder from Japanese groceries, but it's very easy to make your own. Simply make several cuts into ½ oz (15 g) of dried kombu seaweed, and soak in 140–150°F (60–65°C) warm water for about one hour. Putting the broth in a heat-retaining pot or water bottle keeps it warm and allows the stock to brew more effectively.

Cutting Methods

How you cut the ingredients will greatly affect the taste and finish of the dish. Enjoy the same vegetable by cutting it in different ways depending on the preparation method, cooking time, and other factors.

❶ Mincing

When eaten raw, minced vegetables are at their most distinctive, but when cooked their strong flavor is removed and their sweetness is more prevalent.

❷ Shredding

When eaten raw, shredded vegetables tend to show their individuality and have a crunchy, crispy texture. When shredded vegetables are cooked, the seasonings soak in more easily and cooking time is relatively quick. Note that vegetables will wilt quickly when they are cooked if they are cut perpendicular to the fibers. This cutting method helps to release moisture and bring out the sweetness of the vegetables.

❸ Cutting up roughly

This means cutting up vegetables unpeeled into rough pieces of approximately the same size. This cutting method works well with root vegetables such as carrots, in simmered dishes. Since the sizes of the randomly shaped pieces are uniform, both the peel and the insides of the vegetables cook uniformly, and flavors penetrate the vegetables evenly.

❹ Cutting into sticks

This cutting method is recommended for solid vegetables such as cucumbers, carrots and celery stalks used in pickles, or in stewed dishes with long heating times. It helps them retain their shape and brings out the flavor of the vegetables.

❺ Dicing

This is a great way to make the most of solid vegetables such as cucumbers, carrots and celery stalks when you want to enjoy their crunchy textures in salads. It's also an easy way to mix and match multiple ingredients.

❻ Ripping

Ripping up leafy vegetables such as cabbage and lettuce into pieces by hand creates more surface area for dressings and sauces to cling to, while still retaining their crispiness when eaten raw. When ripped-up leafy vegetables are cooked with heat, the flavors soak into them more easily.

Glossary of Japanese Ingredients

All ingredients listed in this glossary can be found at Japanese or Asian markets or at online retailers of Japanese and Asian foods. Fresh vegetables can often be found in local farmers' markets.

Aburaage, sometimes called "fried-skin tofu" is a ready-fried thin sheet of tofu.

Amazake is a sweet, fermented, low-alcohol rice wine often used for cooking and preserving. You can find it readymade in Japanese markets, or you can make it yourself following the recipe on page 9.

Asian pear, called *nashi* in Japanese, is sweet and juicy and crisper than a Western pear.

Atsuage is a tofu block that is sold deep-fried. The outside has a thick, chewy layer and the inside remains creamy.

Bitter melon, called *goya* in Japanese, looks like a prickly cucumber. Bitter in taste, it is filled with nutrients. It is a popular food in Japan's tropical island chain of Okinawa where life expectancy is one of the longest in the world.

Burdock root is a long brown fibrous root with a strong aroma and crunchy texture.

Chinese yam is called *nagaimo* in Japanese and is widely sold in Asian markets. It is a long, light beige root with a watery texture. When grated it has a soft, viscous quality.

Chrysanthemum greens have a crunchy texture and sweet, grassy flavor. Eat them raw or cooked. If you can't find chrysanthemum greens, substitute with watercress or arugula.

Daikon radish This Japanese staple root vegetable is now widely available in regular supermarkets. Spicy and crunchy when raw, it turns soft and sweet when cooked.

Eggplant The eggplants used in this book are the long, thin Asian variety. They are usually sweeter, more tender and have fewer seeds than the large round Western variety.

Enoki mushrooms are long and thin and come in clumps attached to a root. They are also known as winter mushrooms or golden needle mushrooms.

Glass noodles or cellophane noodles are called *harusame* in Japanese. Transparent, they are made from starch and water, and sold dried.

Gyoza dumpling wrappers are sold in thin rounds. They are similar to Chinese potsticker wrappers but thinner, and may only be available in Japanese markets.

Komatsuna is a green leafy vegetable also known as Japanese mustard spinach. If you can't find it, you can substitute any type of mustard green.

Kombu seaweed is an umami-packed ingredient used for stocks and in pickling. It is sold in dried sheets and is becoming widely available in regular Western supermarkets.

Kudzu powder is a starch used for thickening, made from the roots of the kudzu plant. It can be substituted with other kinds of starches such as cornflour or arrowroot.

Mirin is a sweet rice liquor. Originally a drink, nowadays it's generally only used for cooking and is a staple in the Japanese kitchen. It adds sweetness and a shiny finish.

Miso is a fermented paste made of soybeans plus wheat or rice, and is becoming widely available in Western supermarkets. Red miso is made mostly with soybeans and is more strongly flavored and saltier than white miso (which is actually light brown). There are many types of miso; if you can't get hold of the particular type I recommend in a recipe, you can use whatever type of miso you prefer or have on hand.

Mizuna mustard greens have jagged leaves and an earthy flavor. You can substitute any kind of mustard green.

Mochi rice is short-grain and glutinous and becomes sticky when cooked. It is used in mochi rice cakes and in other traditional Japanese dishes.

Nameko mushrooms are small, orange-brown mushrooms with a gelatinous texture. They are sometimes available fresh in Asian markets, and also canned or bottled. Shiitake can be substituted.

Natto is cooked and fermented soybeans. It's rather pungent and can be an acquired taste, but is highly nutritious and worth getting to like.

Okara is soybean pulp, a by-product of the tofu-making process, called "tofu lees" or "tofu dregs" in English. You may find it fresh at Japanese or Korean markets, or you can source it from a tofu maker if you happen to know one.

Ra-yu chili oil sometimes called "la-yu" chili oil in English is an aromatic sesame oil that has been infused with chili peppers. You can find it in a Japanese market, or replace with any kind of chili oil.

Rice Short-grain Japonica rice is used in all the recipes in this book that call for rice. When sold in the West it is sometimes labeled "sushi rice."

Rice koji is also known as "malted rice" in English. It is ready-fermented rice and is available fresh or dried.

Rice vinegar is widely used in Japanese cuisine as a seasoning and a dressing.

Sake lees called *sake kasu* in Japanese are a by-product of the sake-making process. It can be bought in dried slabs or in paste form, and sometimes as a powder.

Sansho pepper is an aromatic, citrusy spice, made from the seed pods of the Japanese prickly-ash tree.

Satsumaimo sweet potato has a dark pink skin and a creamy yellow flesh. It is rich in vitamins C and E, as well as in potassium and copper. If you can't find satsumaimo, any sweet potato can be substituted.

Shiitake mushrooms are used both fresh and dried in Japanese cuisine. Most recipes use only the cap, as the stem is tough and fibrous.

Shimeji mushrooms are also called beech mushrooms and come in white or brown varieties—either color is fine for the recipes in this book. They grow in clumps, are hard and bitter when raw, but softer and tastier when cooked.

Shio koji is often called "rice malt seasoning" in English. It is a fermented mix of rice koji, salt and water. It is sold in paste form and is found in the refrigerated sections of Japanese markets.

Shiso leaves are called "perilla" in English. They come in red or green varieties. Basil is a decent substitute if you can't get hold of shiso.

Umeboshi are salt-pickled ume plums, related to apricots. Use the large, fleshy variety for the recipes in this book.

Ume vinegar is the brine produced when making umeboshi pickled plums. It is often labeled "ume plum vinegar" when sold in the West.

Taro root is a small, round starchy vegetable with a fibrous skin.

Turnips Small, white Japanese turnips are milder and sweeter than the Western variety, but very young and fresh Western turnips would also work well for the recipes in this book.

Yuzu is a tart citrus fruit native to Japan. If you can't find it, use lemon or lime instead.

Making the Most of Your Vegetables

Salt-steamed Green Beans

All you have to do is sprinkle the green beans with salt and steam them.
This recipe is really simple, but surprisingly delicious.

AN EASY-TO-MAKE AMOUNT

30–50 green beans, about
  10 oz (300 g)
Salt, for sprinkling
¼ cup (60 ml) water

❶ Remove the tops and strings
from the green beans.
❷ Place the green beans in a
heavy saucepan (preferably
a cast iron enameled pot),
sprinkle them with a little less
than a teaspoon of salt, and
rub it in well.
❸ Pour in the water, cover the
pan and place over low-medium heat. Stir occasionally, adding a little more water if the
pan becomes dry and the green
beans are still firm but not
moist. When the beans begin
to turn bright green, increase
the heat a little to evaporate
the water, then remove from
the heat.

Green Bean Japchae

This is my version of japchae, a popular Korean noodle dish. Slowly cooking the green beans softens their distinctive taste, and the addition of garlic and sesame oil amps up the flavors.

SERVES 2

10–15 green beans, about 3½ oz (100 g)
¾ oz (20 g) dried glass noodles
White sesame seeds, to taste
Soy sauce, to taste
Sesame oil, to taste
1 tablespoon sesame oil
½ garlic clove, peeled and grated
Salt, to taste

A Ingredients
1 heaping teaspoon ground sesame seeds
1 tablespoon soy sauce
1 teaspoon mirin
Pinch of ground chili pepper
2 tablespoons water

❶ Top and tail the green beans, remove the strings and cut the beans in half. Cook the glass noodles following the packet directions, drain and cut into bite-size pieces. Sprinkle the noodles with soy sauce and sesame oil.

❷ Put the 1 tablespoon of sesame oil and the garlic in a frying pan and sauté over low heat until fragrant. Add the green beans, reduce the heat to medium and sauté until the green beans are sweet. Stir in the A Ingredients and cook until the liquid is reduced.

❸ Add the glass noodles from Step 1, season with salt to taste and arrange on a plate.

NOTE

Making the most of green beans

The key to delicious green beans is to soften them by rubbing with salt before cooking, or simply cook them until they are softened and wilted. Cooking the green beans whole without cutting into pieces, and steaming rather than boiling will help concentrate the umami flavors.

Snow Peas with Chili Oil

The only ingredients used in this dish are snow peas, salt and chili oil. Snow peas are usually added as a colorful garnish to dishes, but here they become the stars of the show. Enjoy their unique crispy texture.

AN EASY-TO-MAKE AMOUNT

80–100 snow peas, about 7 oz (200 g)
1 teaspoon salt

A Ingredients
½ teaspoon salt
A little ra-yu chili oil

1 Remove the tops and strings from the snow peas. Sprinkle them with the teaspoon of salt and rub it in lightly. Boil quickly in a small amount of water.
2 Sprinkle the snow peas with the A Ingredients while still hot, and serve.

Sugar Snap Pea Salad with Ume Dressing

This pea-only salad uses thirty whole sugar snap peas! The sweetness of the sugar snap peas is enhanced by the ume plum–flavored dressing.

AN EASY-TO-MAKE AMOUNT

30 sugar snap peas, about 7 oz (200 g)
1½ teaspoons salt, divided

For the Ume Dressing
2 umeboshi plums, or to taste, pitted and minced
2 tablespoons finely chopped sweet onion
2 tablespoons olive oil
1 tablespoon maple syrup
1 teaspoon rice vinegar
1 teaspoon soy sauce

1 Remove the tops and strings from the sugar snap peas, sprinkle with 1 teaspoon salt and rub it in lightly. Cook for about 1 minute in boiling water, drain into a colander, and sprinkle with ½ teaspoon salt.

2 Mix all the Ume Dressing ingredients well before combining with the sugar snap peas. Arrange in a serving bowl.

Kabocha Squash Spring Rolls

With their sweet and salty flavors and fragrance of green shiso, these spring rolls can be served as a main course with rice or as a drinking snack.

MAKES 10 SPRING ROLLS

¼ kabocha squash, about 14 oz (400 g), after pith and seeds are removed
1 teaspoon salt
½ cup (120 ml) water
10 green shiso leaves
10 spring roll wrappers
Flour, for sealing
Canola oil, for frying

❶ Roughly chop the squash with the skin on. Place the squash in a heavy pot together with 1 teaspoon salt and ½ cup of water. Cover with a lid and cook the squash over low heat. When the squash is almost completely soft, raise the heat and evaporate the remaining moisture, and mash it using a potato masher while it's still hot. Divide into 10 portions.

❷ Spread out the 10 spring roll wrappers. Place a shiso leaf on each wrapper, and spread out a portion of mashed kabocha thinly on top. Fold the left and right sides of the wrapper towards the center, and roll up the wrapper from the bottom to top. Spread a little flour dissolved in water on the seam of the wrapper and seal.

❸ Put ½–1 inch of canola oil in a frying pan, and shallow-fry the spring rolls until crispy.

Pan-fried Turnips with Sesame

The turnips are pan-fried to bring out their sweetness, and sesame seeds add a natural richness. The green turnip tops are also used, so nothing is wasted.

AN EASY-TO-MAKE AMOUNT

5 small Asian turnips with the green tops on, approx 3 inches (7.5 cm) diameter, about 3¼ lbs (1.5 kg) total
Pinch of salt

A Ingredients
6½ tablespoons ground white sesame seeds
3 tablespoons soy sauce
2 tablespoons rice vinegar
1 tablespoon ginger juice (extract by squeezing out grated ginger)
Salt, to taste

❶ Cut the green tops off the turnips and reserve. Cut each turnip lengthwise into 8 equal wedges. Briefly blanch the turnip greens in boiling water with a pinch of salt. Transfer the greens to cold water, squeeze out well and cut into 1 inch (2.5 cm) pieces.
❷ Heat a dry heavy frying pan over medium heat. Spread the turnip pieces in the frying pan and fry until browned on every side.
❸ Mix the A Ingredients, the greens and the turnips together gently so the turnips do not fall apart.

NOTE
Making the most of turnips

The small Asian turnips used in this recipe have different flavors depending on the season. Spring turnips are best eaten raw, while fall turnips are delicious both raw and cooked. However, turnips have a light flavor, so they benefit from being combined with other ingredients. Sesame seeds are a good match, and so is abu-raage fried tofu skin. You can also grate and steam turnips or heat them in a blender to make a creamy soup.

Cauliflower Soup with Soy Milk and Sake Lees

Cauliflower, often disliked for its mushy texture, makes a deliciously rich soup, which is a great way to up your intake of this nutritious vegetable.

SERVES 2

¼ –½ cauliflower, about 7 oz (200 g)
¼ onion
Italian parsley, to taste
1 generous tablespoon canola oil
1 cup (240 ml) water
Italian parsley, to serve

A Ingredients
2 tablespoons sake lees
¾ cup (200 ml) unsweetened soy milk
Scant 1 teaspoon salt

❶ Divide the cauliflower into small florets. Slice the onion thinly lengthwise.
❷ Heat the canola oil in a heavy saucepan, add the onion and sauté slowly over medium heat until slightly browned. Add the cauliflower and sauté some more, then add 1 cup of water and cook while stirring until the cauliflower is soft.
❸ Put the Step 2 and A Ingredients in a blender (or use a stick blender) and blend. Return the mixture to the pan and warm up over medium heat. Ladle into bowls and scatter with Italian parsley.

Korean-style Mustard Green Salad

This takes its inspiration from saengchae, a Korean raw-vegetable dish. Mustard greens with tender stems meant for salad work well here. Pairing spicy mustard greens with a spicy chili dressing gives an extra kick!

1 bunch tender mustard greens, about 5½ oz (150 g)

A Ingredients
2 tablespoons soy sauce
1½ tablespoons roasted white sesame seeds
1½ tablespoons sesame oil
Pinch of chili pepper powder
Pinch of salt

❶ Cut the mustard greens into 2 inch (5 cm) pieces.
❷ Combine the A Ingredients, mix with the mustard greens, and serve.

NOTE — Making the most of mustard greens

It can be difficult to find interesting ways to serve spicy mustard greens. When buying, look for the ones marketed as suitable for salad, which have softer stems and are more enjoyable to eat. As in the recipe on this page, the distinctive, spicy flavor can be balanced by dressing with strong-flavored seasonings such as sesame oil or chili. In the vegetable garden, try to avoid harvesting too much at a time by staggering the sowing of seeds, or share the mustard greens with your neighbors instead of forcing yourself to eat them all!

Miso and Mushroom Stuffed Cabbage

A whole cabbage is stuffed with aburaage deep-fried tofu and shiitake mushrooms, which give a meaty texture. These simple vegetable ingredients make a satisfying main dish.

AN EASY-TO-MAKE AMOUNT

1 small cabbage, about 2 lb 4 oz (1 kg)
2½ cups (600 ml) kombu dashi stock (see page 11)
2–3 tablespoons kudzu powder; adjust the amount depending on the amount of cooking liquid left

For the Miso Filling

3 sheets aburaage deep-fried tofu skins
5 fresh shiitake mushrooms
½ inch (1 cm) piece ginger
6½ tablespoons barley miso, or a mild, rice-based miso

① Remove the leaves from the cabbage one by one and stack up in their original order.(It is okay if they get torn).

② To make the filling, finely mince the aburaage, shiitake mushrooms and ginger, and mix well with the miso.

③ Spread a little of the filling on top of each cabbage leaf (it is not necessary to cover the entire leaf), keeping the leaves stacked up on top of each other as if you were re-assembling the cabbage. When the cabbage shape has been re-formed, wrap it with cooking twine in a crisscross pattern and tie tightly.

④ Place the stuffed cabbage and the kombu dashi stock in a pan, place a heavy plate or lid right on top of the cabbage to act as a weight, and turn the heat to medium. When the stock comes to a boil, turn the heat to low and simmer for about 30 minutes.

⑤ Take out the cabbage and remove the cooking twine. Cut into quarters, and arrange on serving plates. Bring the cooking liquid to a boil, gradually add the kudzu powder dissolved in the same amount of water as the flour (1 tablespoon of flour to 1 tablespoon of water), stir to thicken, and pour over the cabbage.

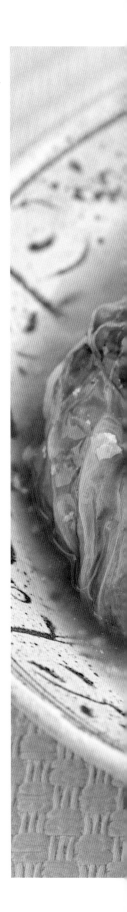

Stir-fried Cabbage and Soybeans with Cumin

Cumin, the main spice in curry powder, is a great side player that enhances the flavor of vegetables. It goes especially well with cabbage, and you'll definitely want second helpings of this dish.

AN EASY-TO-MAKE AMOUNT

½ small cabbage, about
   1 lb 2 oz (500 g)
1½ tablespoons olive oil
1 tablespoon cumin seeds
1 cup (170 g) cooked canned
   soybeans
1 teaspoon salt

❶ Cut cabbage and its stem into rough chunks.
❷ Heat the olive oil and cumin seeds in a frying pan over low heat until the oil is bubbling and fragrant, then add the cabbage and soybeans and sauté over medium heat.
❸ When the cabbage is wilted, season with the salt, and serve.

TIP: Canned soybeans are available at Japanese grocery stores. Try substituting other ready-cooked canned beans too, such as chickpeas.

Nepalese Cucumber Curry

Cucumbers are usually eaten raw, but are actually delicious cooked. The volume of the cucumber reduces during the cooking process, so this is an easy and tasty way to increase your vegetable intake.

SERVES 2

4–5 small Asian cucumbers, about 1 lb 2 oz (500 g) total
1 medium tomato
½ onion
2 tablespoons olive oil
1 teaspoon cumin seeds
1 garlic clove, peeled and finely minced
1 tablespoon curry powder
1 cup (240 ml) water
1 teaspoon salt, plus more to taste
1 teaspoon soy sauce

❶ Cut the cucumbers and tomato roughly into large chunks, and slice the onion thinly lengthwise.

❷ Place the olive oil and the cumin seeds in a heavy saucepan over low heat. Sauté until fragrant, about 1 minute, then add the onion and garlic, reduce the heat to medium and sauté until slightly browned.

❸ Add the cucumbers and sauté for 2–3 minutes. Add the curry powder and tomato in that order, and sauté for another minute.

❹ Pour in the cup of water, bring to a boil, cover and simmer for 5 minutes. Add 1 teaspoon each of salt and soy sauce. Reduce the heat to low and simmer for a further 2–3 minutes. Taste and adjust with a pinch of salt if necessary.

Whole Browned Cucumbers with Salsa

This eye-catching dish is made by cooking eight small cucumbers whole. The cucumbers are cooked until browned and then served with a spicy topping of salsa.

AN EASY-TO-MAKE AMOUNT

8 small Asian cucumbers, about 1 lb 12 oz (800 g) total
½ teaspoon salt
⅓ teaspoon pepper
Flour, for dredging
1½ –2 tablespoons olive oil

For the Salsa

14 oz (400 g) tomatoes or cherry tomatoes, cut into ¼ inch (5 mm) dice
1 red onion, finely minced
1–2 jalapeño peppers, or chili powder, to taste
2 tablespoons lemon juice
2 tablespoons maple syrup
2 tablespoons light soy sauce
2 teaspoons salt
Finely minced fresh coriander, to taste

❶ Sprinkle the cucumbers with the salt and pepper, then dredge them in a thin layer of flour using a tea strainer. Mix the salsa ingredients well.

❷ Heat 1½–2 tablespoons olive oil in a frying pan over medium heat, place the cucumbers in the pan and cover, rolling them over occasionally to brown them all over nicely.

❸ Arrange the cucumbers on a serving plate and put plenty of salsa over them. Cut into bite-size pieces before serving.

NOTE — Making the most of cucumber

Cucumber goes well with all kinds of foods, and most people are likely to eat it raw in salads. However, I recommend cooking cucumber. You can do this in a variety of ways, such as grilling, stir-frying, stewing in curry or other dishes, or as a filling for gyoza dumplings. By rubbing with salt and squeezing out excess moisture beforehand, or pan-frying slowly, you can accentuate the delicious texture of this unexpectedly versatile vegetable.

Crunchy Bitter Melon Rings

The distinctive bitterness of bitter melon becomes milder when it is deep-fried.
By cutting the vegetable into rings and coating with breadcrumbs,
the outside turns crispy while the inside is deliciously juicy.

AN EASY-TO-MAKE AMOUNT

**1 bitter melon, about 9 oz
(250 g)**
Oil, for deep-frying
Salt, to serve

For the Coating
Flour
Grated Chinese yam
Panko breadcrumbs

❶ Cut both ends off the bitter melon, and take out the seeds and pith from the inside by poking it with chopsticks. Cut into ½ inch (1 cm) rounds.
❷ Coat the bitter melon rounds with flour, grated Chinese yam, and panko breadcrumbs, in that order.
❸ In a frying pan, heat about 1 inch (2.5 cm) of oil to between 340–360ºF (170–180ºC), then deep-fry the bitter melon until golden brown. Arrange on a serving plate with salt to dip the rings in.

Crispy Burdock Chips

Burdock root is a long brown vegetable with a great aroma and crunchy texture. You can find it at Asian groceries and farmers' markets. A little work is required to soften and cook the burdock root before deep-frying, but the taste is worth it.

AN EASY-TO-MAKE AMOUNT

2 burdock roots, about 10 oz (300 g) total
¾ cup (200 ml) water
3 tablespoons soy sauce, or to taste
Oil, for deep-frying

For the Coating
½ cup (60 g) flour
1 teaspoon five spice powder
1 teaspoon grated garlic

1 Wash the burdock well, and cut into 2 inch (5 cm) pieces. Put the burdock in a heavy-bottomed pan with a quarter to a half of the water (adjust the amount depending on the size of the pan). Cover with a lid and simmer over low heat until tender. Raise the heat to high to evaporate the excess water, then sprinkle with the soy sauce.

2 Combine all the coating ingredients in a bowl and mix. Add the burdock root and mix again.

3 Heat the oil to between 340–360°F (170–180°C). Put in the coated burdock root pieces 2 or 3 at a time, and deep-fry until golden brown.

Gyoza Dumplings with Komatsuna

Komatsuna mustard greens are packed with umami flavor, making it hard to believe that these dumplings are only filled with vegetables. If you can't find komatsuna, substitute any leafy green vegetable of your choice.

MAKES 25 DUMPLINGS

1 bunch komatsuna, about 7 oz (200 g)
Pinch of salt
5 fresh shiitake mushrooms
4 inch (10 cm) piece leek or fat green onion
25 gyoza dumpling wrappers
1 tablespoon sesame oil
1 cup (240 ml) water

A Ingredients
1 tablespoon finely minced ginger
2 heaping tablespoons flour
1 teaspoon sesame oil
½ teaspoon salt
A little soy sauce
A little pepper

For the Dipping Sauce
Vinegar, soy sauce, ra-yu chili oil

1 Cut off the root ends of the komatsuna and boil in plenty of hot water with a pinch of salt for 30 seconds to 1 minute. Drain and put into cold water. Drain, squeeze out the excess water thoroughly, and chop. Discard the hard stem ends from the shiitake mushrooms and finely mince the caps. Finely mince the leek or green onion. Put all of the above into a bowl, add the A Ingredients and mix well.
2 Place 25 equal portions of the Step 1 mixture on each gyoza skin, fold the skin in half, and squeeze the edges together. Combine the dipping sauce ingredients.

3 Heat the 1 tablespoon of sesame oil in a frying pan. Line up the filled dumplings from Step 2 in the pan with the flat sides down and fry until a light golden brown. Add 1 cup of water, cover the pan with a lid and steam-fry.
4 When there is almost no moisture left in the pan take the lid off, and cook until all the moisture has evaporated. Arrange on a serving plate with the sauce from Step 2.

Komatsuna Ohitashi with Chinese Yam

Ohitashi is a Japanese dish where lightly cooked vegetables are served cold with a sauce. This version uses two whole bunches of komatsuna mustard greens, but by adding grated Chinese yam as a topping, it becomes something out of the ordinary. This dish has a pleasingly smooth texture.

AN EASY-TO-MAKE AMOUNT

**2 bunches komatsuna, about
  14 oz (400 g)
Pinch of salt
¾ cup (200 ml) grated Chinese yam
A little grated wasabi, to serve**

A Ingredients
**¾ cup (200 ml) kombu dashi stock
  (see page 11)
2 tablespoons soy sauce**

❶ Cut off the root ends of the komatsuna and boil in plenty of hot water with a pinch of salt for 30 seconds to 1 minute. Drain and put into cold water. Drain again into a colander and squeeze out the excess water. Cut into 2 inch (5 cm) pieces. Put into a shallow container.
❷ Combine the A Ingredients, pour over the komatsuna in the container and leave to marinate for about 10 minutes.
❸ Transfer the komatsuna with the sauce and pour the grated Chinese yam over it. Top with a little wasabi.

NOTE

Making the most of komatsuna

Like any green leafy vegetable, komatsuna is good for you, but it can be a bit boring if served alone or served too often. One way to make this (and other nutritious leafy greens) more interesting is to serve with a topping of grated Chinese yam. The yam's smooth texture has a great mouthfeel and really enhances the taste of the komatsuna. My family in Japan were farmers of Chinese yam—*nagaimo*, as it's called in Japanese—and we used to pour grated Chinese yam over food that we were tired of or didn't enjoy eating. That's where the inspiration for this recipe came from!

Sweet Potato in Spicy Sichuan Sauce

This spicy style of cooking—called mapo or mabo in Japan—is from China's Sichuan Province. This dish is usually made with ground meat and tofu or eggplant. Here, I've used shiitake and walnuts for a meat-like texture.

AN EASY-TO-MAKE AMOUNT

1 large Japanese satsumaimo sweet potato, about 12 oz (350 g)
½ cup (120 ml) water
Pinch of salt
1 tablespoon sesame oil
¼ large green onion, minced

Small piece ginger, finely minced
5 shiitake mushrooms, finely minced
2 tablespoons finely chopped unsalted walnuts
1½ teaspoons kudzu powder
Finely minced green onion, for garnish

A Ingredients

1 red chili pepper, seeds removed and sliced
1½ tablespoons miso, or to taste
1½ tablespoons soy sauce
¾ cup (200 ml) kombu dashi stock (see page 11)

❶ Wash the sweet potato and cut into ½ inch (1.5 cm) cubes, leaving the skin on. Place in a heavy pan, and add ¼–½ cup water (depending on the size of the pan) and a pinch of salt. Put the lid on tightly, and steam-cook over low heat until the potato is tender. Remove the lid, turn the heat up and evaporate the water.

❷ In a deep frying pan, heat the tablespoon of sesame oil over medium-low heat, add the green onion and ginger, and sauté until they begin to brown. Turn the heat to medium and add the shiitake mushrooms, walnuts and the combined A Ingredients. Simmer for about 3 minutes.

❸ Dissolve the kudzu powder in 1½ teaspoons of water and gradually add to the frying pan to thicken the mixture. Finally, add the sweet potato to the pan and mix.

❹ Serve sprinkled with the minced green onion.

Pan-fried Taro Root with Herbed Breadcrumbs

Taro root is a popular ingredient in traditional Japanese dishes,
but this recipe uses olive oil, garlic and parsley for a delicious European twist.

AN EASY-TO-MAKE AMOUNT

6 taro roots, about 1 lb 2 oz (500 g) total
Olive oil, for sprinkling
Salt, for sprinkling

A Ingredients

½ cup (30 g) panko bread-crumbs
2 tablespoons olive oil
2 tablespoons finely minced parsley
1 tablespoon finely minced garlic
½ teaspoon salt

1 Peel the taro roots and cut into ¾ inch (2 cm) slices. Sprinkle with olive oil and a little salt.
2 Preheat the oven to 400ºF (200ºC). Place the taro root slices on a baking sheet lined with kitchen parchment paper, and bake for about 10 minutes until a bamboo skewer goes through a slice easily.
3 Combine the A Ingredients and spoon on top of the taro root slices. Turn the oven temperature to 430ºF (230ºC) and bake for a further 5–7 minutes until lightly browned.

Pressed Sushi with Tofu and Shiso Leaves

With only two main ingredients, this is a surprisingly tasty dish, with a refreshing aroma from the shiso. This is great to serve on a hot summer day.

AN EASY-TO-MAKE AMOUNT

20–30 green shiso leaves
½ teaspoon salt
1 piece aburaage fried tofu skin
1¾ cups (330 g) warm cooked Japanese short-grain rice
1 tablespoon ume vinegar

A Ingredients
3½ tablespoons kombu dashi stock (see page 11)
2 teaspoons soy sauce
2 teaspoons mirin

❶ Finely shred the shiso leaves, rub them with the salt, then squeeze out the excess moisture.
❷ Finely mince the aburaage. Place in a frying pan and sauté lightly over medium heat. Add the A Ingredients and simmer until there is no moisture left in the pan.
❸ Combine the rice with the ume vinegar.
❹ Line a pressed sushi mold or a small shallow rectangular container about 2¼ x 5½ inches (6 cm x 14 cm) with plastic wrap. Line the bottom of the container with half the shiso, half the rice and half the aburaage in that order, then repeat with the rest of the shiso, rice and aburaage. Press down firmly.
❺ Take the sushi out of the container and take off the plastic wrap. Cut into easy-to-eat pieces.

Potatoes Baked with Sansho Pepper

The skins of potatoes are delicious too, so cook them whole and unpeeled. The salt and sansho pepper mix is the perfect accompaniment and makes these simple potatoes really irresistible.

TIP: Sansho pepper is available at Japanese grocery stores. It is similar to but milder than Sichuan pepper.

AN EASY-TO-MAKE AMOUNT

1 teaspoon sansho pepper
1 teaspoon salt
2 tablespoons canola oil or sesame oil
5–6 medium potatoes, about 2 lb 4 oz (1 kg)

❶ Mix the sansho pepper and salt, and reserve some of it to use for dipping. Combine the rest of it with the oil and mix well.

❷ Wash the potatoes (do not peel) and coat with the salt, pepper and oil mixture. Wrap each potato in aluminum foil.

❸ Preheat the oven to 430ºF (230ºC) and bake the wrapped potatoes for 50 minutes to 1 hour, until a skewer goes through one easily.

❹ Serve the potatoes with the reserved salt and pepper mix, to dip into as you eat.

NOTE

Making the most of potatoes

Potatoes are best cooked whole because the skin is full of umami. Boiling, baking, or steaming potatoes whole in their skins will concentrate this umami without losing any of it—if you are using potatoes with other ingredients as part of another recipe, this preparation will allow other flavors to soak in quickly and easily. The mild taste of potatoes means that you can have fun adding flavorful accents such as pepper, garlic, chili and other spices.

Buchimgae with Chrysanthemum Greens

Buchimgae is a Korean pancake—my version is made using one whole bunch of chrysanthemum greens. By keeping the amount of flour to a minimum, you can enjoy the unique flavor of the greens.

AN EASY-TO-MAKE AMOUNT

5½ oz (150 g) chrysanthemum greens
2 tablespoons sesame oil

For the Batter

¾ cup (80 g) flour
2 tablespoons potato starch or cornstarch
Pinch of salt
6½ tablespoons water

For the Sauce

1 tablespoon finely minced green onion
2 teaspoons ground sesame seeds
2 tablespoons soy sauce
2 tablespoons rice vinegar
Pinch of chili pepper powder

❶ Cut the chrysanthemum greens into 2 inch (5 cm) long pieces. If the stems are thick, bash them with a rolling pin or the side of your knife to help them cook through.

❷ Put the chrysanthemum greens into a bowl, and add the batter ingredients in the order listed. Mix well.

❸ Put the 2 tablespoons sesame oil in a frying pan and heat over medium heat. Pour the Step 2 mixture into the frying pan to form a pancake shape. Turn the pancake over several times while pressing down on it with a spatula, and brown both sides.

❹ Mix the sauce ingredients together.

❺ Cut the pancake into bite-size pieces, and serve with the sauce on the side.

Thai Som Tam Zucchini

Som tam is a salad from southeast Asia that is made with green papaya. Here I've used zucchini instead, to give the same fresh and crunchy texture.

AN EASY-TO-MAKE AMOUNT

1–2 zucchini, about 7 oz (200 g) total
Scant ½ teaspoon salt
1 green chili pepper
1 tablespoon chopped roasted peanuts (chop with the skins on)

A Ingredients
1½ tablespoons lemon juice
½ tablespoon light soy sauce
2 teaspoons maple syrup
Scant ½ teaspoon salt

❶ Cut the zucchini into ¼ inch (5 mm) thick diagonal slices, then cut each slice into thin strips. Sprinkle with the salt, leave until wilted, and then squeeze out the excess moisture. Remove the top and seeds from the green chili pepper and mince.

❷ Add the chili pepper to the A Ingredients, then add the zucchini and chopped peanuts and mix.

Daikon Radish Gochujang Stew

This is another Korean-inspired recipe that uses a whole daikon radish. The daikon is cut into large pieces to make the most of the umami and sweetness of the skin. Tomato purée adds even more tasty umami.

AN EASY-TO-MAKE AMOUNT

1 daikon radish, about 2 lb 4 oz (1 kg)
Salt, for rubbing
½ cup (120 ml) water

A Ingredients
5 tablespoons soy sauce
2½ tablespoons tomato purée
2 tablespoons gochujang (Korean spicy bean paste)
2 garlic cloves, peeled and grated
2 teaspoons sesame oil

❶ Wash the daikon well, cut off both ends, and cut into 2 inch (5 cm) thick slices, with the skin on. Make ¾ inch (2 cm) deep crisscross cuts into one side of each slice.

❷ Line the bottom of a heavy pan with the daikon slices, and rub the tops and sides with a little salt. Add ½ cup of water to the pan, turn the heat to very low and steam-cook the daikon, covered, for about 20 minutes. Turn the slices over and steam-cook for another 20 minutes. The daikon is done when a skewer goes through a piece easily, and the water level has reduced down to about a quarter of the height of the slices. If the water boils down too low while the daikon is cooking, add a little more.

❸ Mix the A Ingredients together and add to the pan. Cover again, and simmer over very low heat for 15 minutes, while basting the daikon with the sauce. Turn the slices over and repeat this process for another 15 minutes. Leave to the daikon to cool in the pan and soak up the flavors. When cool, arrange on a serving plate and spoon the sauce over.

NOTE — Making the most of daikon radish

Since daikon radish has a high water content for a root vegetable, removing that water reduces its bulk and allows you to eat more of it. The key is to let the moisture drain out slowly. The gochujang stew on this page is made by slow steaming, and the Herb-roasted Daikon on page 44 is made by slow roasting, which draws out the moisture. Daikon adapts itself well to a wide variety of seasonings, so you can experiment with preparing it in different ways.

Herb-roasted Daikon

This dish maximizes the juiciness of the daikon by roasting it whole in its skin. For a surprisingly flavorful alternative, try seasoning just with salt and pepper.

AN EASY-TO-MAKE AMOUNT

1 small daikon radish, about 1 lb 10 oz (750 g)

A Ingredients
2 tablespoons olive oil
1 teaspoon salt
Coarsely ground black pepper, to taste
1 garlic clove, peeled and grated
1–2 sprigs fresh rosemary

1 Wash the daikon well, and cut it to fit the length of the baking sheet you will use in Step 2. Place the daikon, unpeeled, on a piece of aluminum foil unpeeled, sprinkle with the A Ingredients in the order listed, and wrap up tightly with the foil.
2 Preheat the oven to 430ºC (230ºC). Line the baking sheet with kitchen parchment paper, place the foil-wrapped daikon on it and bake for about 1 hour, or until a skewer goes through it easily.
3 Open up the foil and cut into 1 inch (2–3 cm) thick slices to eat.

Daikon Pepper Steaks

Daikon radish slices are first dried and then slowly cooked to remove the moisture, a process that concentrates the umami. This dish is so delicious that it's hard to believe it's seasoned with only salt and pepper.

AN EASY-TO-MAKE AMOUNT

1 daikon radish, about 2 lb 4 oz (1 kg)
Salt, to taste
Coarsely ground black pepper, to taste
1½–2 tablespoons olive oil

1 Wash the daikon well, cut into 1 inch (2.5 cm) slices with the skin left on, and dry in the sun for 4–5 days.

2 Season both sides of the slices lightly with salt and coarsely ground black pepper. Heat the olive oil in a frying pan, place the daikon slices in the pan, cover and cook over low heat. When browned, turn and cook slowly for a further 30 minutes until the center is cooked through.

3 Arrange on a serving plate and sprinkle with coarsely ground black pepper.

Daikon Katsu

The coating is crispy and the inside is juicy for an unexpected taste sensation! These veggie katsu cutlets are as satisfying as the meat versions and can be served with rice as a main meal, or as a snack with drinks.

SERVES 2

2¼ inch (6 cm) long piece daikon radish, about 10 oz (300 g)
½ cup (120 ml) water
Pinch of salt
Vegetable oil, for deep-frying
Japanese karashi mustard, or English mustard, to serve

A Ingredients
2¼ tablespoons soy sauce
1 teaspoon ginger juice (extract by squeezing out grated ginger)

Coating
Flour
Grated Chinese yam
Panko breadcrumbs

❶ Cut the daikon in half lengthwise, then cut into ¾ inch (2 cm) slices leaving the skin on. Put the ½ cup of water and the pinch of salt into a heavy pan. Add the daikon slices, put the lid on and cook over medium heat.

❷ When the pan comes to a boil, turn the heat to low and steam-cook for 15–20 minutes until the daikon is tender. Remove the lid, turn up the heat to evaporate the moisture, then take the pan off the heat to cool.

❸ Put the cooked daikon in a plastic bag with the A Ingredients. Push out all the air and close up the bag. Leave to marinate for about 10 minutes, turning the bag from time to time.

❹ Drain the daikon slices and pat them dry with paper towels. Coat by dipping first in the flour, then in the grated Chinese yam, and finally in the panko breadcrumbs. Heat the oil to between 340–360ºF (170–180ºC) and deep-fry the daikon slices until crispy. Arrange on serving plates with mustard on the side.

Sweet and Salty Onions with Pressed Barley

Sweet and salty onions are a familiar taste in Japanese cuisine, but the fluffy, chewy texture of pressed barley takes an old favorite to a whole new level!

AN EASY-TO-MAKE AMOUNT

2 onions, about 14 oz (400 g) total
1½ tablespoons sesame oil
3 tablespoons pressed or rolled barley
1¼ cups (300 ml) water
3 tablespoons soy sauce
3 tablespoons mirin
Finely chopped green onion, for garnish

❶ Peel the onions and cut each into 8 wedges. Heat the sesame oil in a frying pan over medium heat, and stir-fry the onions slowly until they are lightly browned.
❷ Add the barley and continue stir-frying. Add the water, cover with a lid and bring to a boil. Turn the heat down to low and simmer for about 15 minutes until the barley is cooked.
❸ Remove the lid and add the soy sauce and mirin. Stir the pan occasionally and simmer over low heat for 3–4 minutes until the flavors are absorbed.
❹ Serve sprinkled with chopped green onions.

Red Onion Lemon Pilaf

Red onion, most often seen in salads, becomes a key pilaf ingredient in this recipe. The refreshing sourness of lemon is a lovely, light touch.

SERVES 2–3

1 red onion, about 7 oz (200 g)
¾ cup (150 g) uncooked Japanese short-grain rice
1 tablespoon olive oil
1 tablespoon lemon juice
½ teaspoon salt
Zest of ¼ lemon (preferably organic), for garnish
Minced parsley, for garnish
Coarsely ground black pepper, to taste

❶ Peel the onion and cut into 8–12 wedges. Wash the rice and drain well.

❷ Heat the olive oil in a frying pan, add the onion and sauté until sweet. Add the rice, and sauté until translucent.

❸ Put the lemon juice in a cup and add water to bring the quantity of liquid to ¾ cup (200 ml). Mix in ½ teaspoon salt.

❹ Put the Step 2 and Step 3 ingredients in a rice cooker and cook on the regular setting. When cooked, fluff up the rice with a rice paddle, and serve garnished with lemon zest, parsley and black pepper.

TIP: If you don't have a rice cooker, put Step 2 and 3 ingredients into a pan and bring to a boil. Put on a tight fitting lid and turn the heat down as low as possible. Cook for 13 to 14 minutes, turn off the heat and let rest for 10 more minutes. Fluff up and serve with garnishes as in Step 4.

Boy Choy and Tofu with Sesame

This dish contains two whole bok choy. Black sesame seeds and tofu add richness to the light flavor of this nutritious vegetable. Quick cooking preserves the crisp texture of the bok choy.

AN EASY-TO-MAKE AMOUNT

2 bok choy, about 14 oz (400 g)
½ block firm tofu, about
   5– 6 oz (140–160 g)
1 tablespoon roasted black
   sesame seeds

A Ingredients

¾ cup (200 ml) kombu dashi
   stock (see page 11)
1 teaspoon salt, or to taste
1 dried red chili pepper

❶ Cut the bok choy horizontally into 2 inch (5 cm) pieces, and cut the stem parts into 2–3 pieces lengthwise. Break the tofu with your hands into easy-to-eat pieces.
❷ Put the A Ingredients into a pan and bring to a boil. Add the bok choy and tofu, and simmer over medium heat for about 2 minutes. Remove from the heat.
❸ Add the black sesame seeds while crushing them between your fingers and mix in. Leave to cool to allow the flavors to penetrate the ingredients

Stir-fried Tomatoes and Natto

Two umami powerhouses, tomatoes and natto fermented soybeans, are combined in this dish. The synergistic effect of these two flavor-laden ingredients makes this an irresistible dish.

AN EASY-TO-MAKE AMOUNT

2 large tomatoes, about 14 oz (400 g)
2 tablespoons olive oil
Pinch of dried red chili pepper
2 packs small bean natto, about 3 oz (80 g)
1 teaspoon salt
Soy sauce, to taste
Black pepper, to taste
Finely minced green onion, for garnish

❶ Cut each tomato into 8 wedges. Heat the olive oil in a frying pan, add the tomatoes, chili pepper and natto and stir-fry over medium heat for about 1 minute. Add 1 teaspoon of salt, and a little soy sauce and black pepper to taste.
❷ Serve garnished with green onion.

Miso-stuffed Baked Tomatoes

Tomatoes are the star of this recipe, with six whole ones used. The flavors produced by the slow oven-roasting will make this a dish you return to time and time again.

SERVES 3–6

6 large tomatoes, about 2½ lbs (1.2 kg)
Flour, for dusting

A Ingredients
10 fresh shiitake mushrooms, finely minced
1 cup (60 g) panko bread-crumbs
5 tablespoons barley miso or sweet rice-based miso
2 tablespoons olive oil

❶ Cut the tops off the tomatoes, and scoop out the insides with a spoon (see tip below). Mix the A Ingredients together.
❷ Dust the insides of the tomatoes lightly with flour, and divide the A mixture equally between each tomato. When the tomatoes are stuffed, place the tops back on.
❸ Preheat the oven to 430ºF (230ºC). Line a baking sheet with kitchen paper, place the stuffed tomatoes on it, and bake for about 20 minutes until they are lightly browned and look delicious.

> **TIP:** Don't throw away the insides of the tomatoes. They can be frozen and kept for use in other dishes, such as stews, sauces or smoothies.

NOTE

Making the most of tomatoes

Although tomatoes are often eaten raw, cooking them really brings out the umami flavor. If you bake them slowly to remove the moisture, the umami and richness are enhanced. The umami flavors of tomatoes means that they go well with miso, soy sauce, dashi stock and other umami ingredients. If you have the time, sun-drying tomatoes for 5 hours or so before grilling, roasting or baking them will further deepen their flavor and richness.

Cherry Tomato and Okara Dip

This Italian-style dip is packed with the umami of cherry tomatoes. For a great texture and a Japanese twist, it uses okara—the pulp of the soybean after the milk has been extracted.

AN EASY-TO-MAKE AMOUNT

12 cherry tomatoes, about 7 oz (200 g)
1 garlic clove
2 tablespoons olive oil
1½ oz (40 g) fresh okara
Parsley, minced, for garnish
French baguette, sliced, to serve

A Ingredients
6½ tablespoons tomato puree
6½ tablespoons water
Red chili pepper powder, to taste

❶ Remove the calyxes from the tomatoes and cut each into 4 lengthwise wedges. Peel and finely mince the garlic.
❷ Heat the olive oil in a frying pan with the garlic, and sauté slowly over low heat until the garlic is lightly colored. Add the okara and cook gently until the moisture has evaporated and it has become crumbly. Add the cherry tomatoes, and stir-fry until everything melds together.
❸ Add the A Ingredients and simmer while stirring until there is little moisture left in the pan. Sprinkle with parsley. Serve with slices of baguette.

Baked Eggplant Dip

This baked eggplant recipe has a great creamy texture that makes it perfect for dips. Here it is served with bread, but it can be used in lots of other ways—try it as a pasta sauce.

AN EASY-TO-MAKE AMOUNT

2–3 slender Asian eggplants, about 7 oz (200 g) total
¼ red onion, about 2 oz (50 g)
½ teaspoon salt
Olive oil, for drizzling
French baguette, sliced, to serve

A Ingredients
4 tablespoons olive oil
Scant 1 tablespoon lemon juice
A little grated garlic

❶ Bake the eggplant in a pre-heated 430–480ºF (230–250ºC) oven until the surface is charred. Peel while the eggplant is hot, cut off the tops and chop up finely.

❷ Finely mince the red onion, sprinkle with the ½ teaspoon salt and leave for 10 minutes. Combine the eggplant, onion and A Ingredients and mix.

❸ Transfer to a serving bowl and drizzle with olive oil. Serve with thinly sliced baguette.

Eggplant Braised with Mushroom Sauce

I use eight whole thin eggplants for this dish. The smooth texture of the mushrooms and the freshness of the garnishes will keep you coming back for more.

AN EASY-TO-MAKE AMOUNT

8 slender Asian eggplants, about 1½ lbs (650 g)
Vegetable oil, for deep-frying
7 oz (200 g) mixed mushrooms such as shiitake, shimeji or maitake (hen of the woods)
1 tablespoon kudzu powder
¾ cup (200 ml) kombu dashi stock (see page 11)
3 tablespoons soy sauce
Finely minced green onions, for garnish
Grated ginger, to serve

1 Cut off the tops of the eggplants, cut the eggplants in half lengthwise, pat dry if needed, and deep-fry in oil at 360°F (180°C). Remove and discard the hard stem ends from the mushrooms, cut the shiitake caps into thin slices, and separate the shimeji and maitake mushrooms into small bunches. Dissolve the kudzu powder in 1 tablespoon of water.

2 Put the mushrooms, kombu dashi stock and soy sauce in a pan over medium heat. When the pan comes to a boil add the kudzu powder and water mixture a little at a time to thicken the sauce. When the sauce has thickened, remove from the heat.

3 Spoon the sauce into a serving bowl and top with the fried eggplants. Garnish with the green onions and serve a little grated ginger on the side.

> ### NOTE
> ## Making the most of eggplant
>
> The eggplant is a versatile vegetable that tastes great whether fried, grilled, stir-fried, pickled or baked. Precooked eggplant will keep for up to 3–4 days and it also freezes well. It's a handy item to have on hand to add to curries or soups. The eggplant recipes in this book use the long thin Asian eggplant that you can find at Japanese or Asian markets.

Mexican-style Eggplant and Okra Stew

Spices and herbs are combined with the umami of tomatoes to create a quick dish with a Mexican flavor. Serve with cold beer or wine.

AN EASY-TO-MAKE AMOUNT

3 slender Asian eggplants, about 9 oz (250 g)
10 okra, about 3½ oz (100 g) total
½ onion
1 garlic clove
2 tablespoons olive oil
1 dried red chili pepper, minced
¾ cup (200 ml) thick unsalted tomato juice
½ teaspoon cumin powder
Scant 1 teaspoon salt
½ teaspoon dried oregano
Fresh coriander, for garnish

❶ Cut the tops off the eggplants and chop roughly. Cut the tops off the okra and cut each into three pieces crosswise. Peel and finely mince the onion and garlic.
❷ Heat the olive oil in a heavy saucepan and sauté the onion and garlic over medium-low heat. Turn the heat to medium and add the eggplant and okra in that order, then add the chili pepper and sauté briefly.
❸ Add the tomato juice, bring to a boil, cover and simmer over low heat for 10 minutes. Add the cumin, the salt and oregano, and simmer for a few minutes. Serve garnished with roughly chopped coriander leaves.

Broccolini Marinated in Kombu

Boiled broccolini is simply sandwiched between sheets of kombu seaweed to marinate it. Serve the marinated broccolini as a side, a snack, a sushi roll ingredient, or try wrapping in yuba tofu sheets and serving as an hors d'oeuvre.

AN EASY-TO-MAKE AMOUNT

2–3 bunches broccolini, about
    1 lb 2 oz (500 g)
Pinch of salt
**4 sheets kombu seaweed, each 10 x
    3 inches (25 x 7.5 cm), if possible
    the Rishiri or Rausu variety**
Soy sauce, to serve
Grated wasabi, to serve
Grated ginger, to serve
Salt, to serve

❶ Boil the broccolini briefly in hot water with a pinch of salt, drain, and squeeze out the excess moisture. Wipe the surface of the kombu seaweed with moistened kitchen paper.
❷ Cut the broccolini to the width of the kombu and place on top of the kombu. Place another piece of kombu on top and another layer of broccolini on top. Repeat the process to make three layers.
❸ Place in an airtight bag, taking care not to let the stack disintegrate, and refrigerate overnight. Serve with soy sauce and wasabi, or soy sauce and grated ginger, or just with salt.

> **NOTE**
>
> ## Making the most of broccolini and other greens
>
> Eating large quantities of green vegetables is good for your health but can be monotonous! But using this kombu seaweed marinating technique will impart deep flavor to your vegetables, as if they had been simmered in a rich stock. The slight bitterness of broccolini, in particular, is really enhanced by the umami of the kombu seaweed. Don't throw the kombu away once you've used it—cut it into small pieces and eat it as a stir-fry or tempura ingredient, which is not only delicious but reduces waste too.

Garlic Chive Dip

Garlic chives are used raw for their distinctive taste. The addition of silken tofu and the richness of the fermented seasoning shio koji give the dish a punchy flavor—it's hard to believe this is made only with vegetables.

AN EASY-TO-MAKE AMOUNT

2 oz (50 g) garlic chives
½ block silken tofu, about 6 oz (160 g)
Crackers or sliced French baguette, to serve

A Ingredients
2 tablespoons olive oil
1 tablespoon shio koji
1 tablespoon rice vinegar

❶ Mince the garlic chives finely. Get rid of excess moisture by putting the minced chives in an uncovered bowl and microwaving for 2 minutes at full power. Then drain.

❷ Put the minced and drained garlic chives and the A Ingredients in a food processor and blend until smooth. Serve with crackers or with thin slices of baguette.

Carrots with Umeboshi Plum

In this refreshing dish, the sourness of the umeboshi plums enhances the sweetness of the carrots and brightens their color.

AN EASY-TO-MAKE AMOUNT

6 small carrots, about 1 lb 12 oz (800 g)
6 large umeboshi plums, preserved red shiso leaves, with a salt content of 20%
1¾ cups (400 ml) water
Soy sauce, to taste

❶ Wash the carrots, and halve lengthwise without peeling. Pit the umeboshi plums and mince the flesh into a paste.
❷ Put the Step 1 ingredients into a pan with the 1¾ cups of water. Cover and bring to a boil over low heat. Let simmer for about 30 minutes until there is almost no moisture left in the pan.
❸ Remove from the heat and add a little soy sauce to taste. Leave to cool and for the flavors to meld together before serving.

Curried Carrots with Cashews

Carrots, which have a natural sweetness, are the main ingredient in this curry. It is crisply flavored with spices and given a mild richness with cashew nuts.

AN EASY-TO-MAKE AMOUNT

3 carrots, about 1 lb (450 g)
8 mushrooms
1 large tomato
**⅔ cup (100 g) unsalted cashew
   nuts**
1 tablespoon olive oil
1 teaspoon cumin seeds
1 garlic clove, peeled and minced
Small piece ginger, minced
1 tablespoon curry powder
1¾ cups (400 ml) water
2 teaspoons maple syrup
2 teaspoons salt
Soy sauce, to taste
Pepper, to taste
Cooked rice, to serve

❶ Cut the carrots, without peeling, into rough bite-size pieces. Halve the mushrooms. Remove the calyx from the tomato and chop the tomato roughly. Chop the cashew nuts in a food processor, or very finely with a knife.

❷ In a pan, heat the olive oil, cumin seeds, garlic and ginger over low heat. When fragrant, add the carrots and mushrooms and sauté over medium heat. Add the curry powder and tomatoes and sauté for another minute or so.

❸ Add the 1¾ cups of water. When the pan comes to a boil, turn down the heat, and simmer until the carrots are soft. Add the finely chopped cashew nuts, maple syrup and salt, mix and simmer for another 2 minutes or so.

❹ Add a little soy sauce and pepper to taste, and serve the curry with rice.

Sesame-flavored Carrot Dip

Tender steamed carrots are combined with sesame paste to make a soft
and fluffy mousse-like dip. It can be made in quantity and frozen for later use.

AN EASY-TO-MAKE AMOUNT

4 carrots, about 1 lb 4 oz (600 g)
½ cup (120 ml) water
Pinch of salt
Vegetable sticks (carrots,
 daikon radish, celery, etc.), to
 serve
Crackers, to serve

A Ingredients
4 tablespoons sesame paste or
 tahini
1 tablespoon olive oil
1 tablespoon lemon juice
1 rounded teaspoon salt
Pinch of curry powder
Soy sauce, to taste
Pinch of black pepper
Pinch of chili powder

❶ Cut the carrots, without peeling, into bite-size pieces. Place
in a heavy pan, add ½ cup water
and a pinch of salt, cover with a
lid and turn the heat to medium.
❷ When the water comes to
a boil turn the heat to low, and
steam-cook until the carrots are
soft for 15–20 minutes. Remove
the lid, turn up the heat and evaporate the moisture in the pan.
Take off the heat and let cool.
❸ Put the cooked carrots into a
food processor with the A Ingredients, and blend to a smooth
paste. Serve in a bowl with vegetable sticks and crackers.

Leek Soup with Mochi Rice Cakes

Well-sautéed leeks are simmered in dashi stock and miso is added to give a caramelized color, similar to French onion soup. Instead of French bread, serve with grilled mochi rice cakes and enjoy it piping hot.

SERVES 2

2 small leeks, about 6 oz (160 g) total
1 tablespoon sesame oil
2 cups (480 ml) kombu dashi stock (see page 11)
3 tablespoons Hatcho miso, or miso of your choice
4 dried rice cakes (mochi cakes)
Sansho pepper powder, to serve
Finely shredded yuzu peel, for garnish

❶ Slice the leek thinly. Heat the sesame oil in a frying pan, add the leek and sauté slowly over low heat.

❷ When the leek is light golden brown, transfer to a pot, add the kombu dashi stock and turn the heat to medium. When the stock comes to a boil, lower the heat and add the miso.

❸ Grill the rice cakes or bake in a toaster oven, divide between serving bowls, and pour in the Step 2 soup. Sprinkle with sansho pepper and yuzu peel.

TIP: You can find square-cut and round mochi rice cakes at a Japanese grocery store. Either one will work in this recipe, but here I have used the square-cut type.

Miso-marinated Green Onion and Grapes

Green onions and grapes are an unexpectedly delicious combination!
Here they are mixed with a traditional Japanese miso-and-vinegar dressing
called nuta. This dish goes really well with a glass of white wine.

AN EASY-TO-MAKE AMOUNT

3½ oz (100 g) green onions
16 large Muscat (or similar)
grapes, about 6½ oz (180 g)

A Ingredients
3 tablespoons Saikyo miso (or
miso of your choice)
2 tablespoons olive oil
2 teaspoons white wine vinegar
Pinch of salt

❶ Quickly blanch the green onions and cut into ¾ inch (2 cm) pieces. Cut the grapes in half.
❷ Combine the Step 1 ingredients with the A Ingredients, divide between individual dishes and serve.

Salt-braised Napa Cabbage

By braising the napa cabbage instead of just steaming or stir-frying, its umami becomes very concentrated and you can really appreciate the flavor.

AN EASY-TO-MAKE AMOUNT

½ napa cabbage, about 2 lb 4 oz (1 kg)
2 teaspoons salt, or to taste
2 tablespoons olive oil

❶ Cut the napa cabbage in half lengthwise to end up with 2 quarter pieces. Lift each layer of leaf one at a time, and sprinkle a little salt on the outside of each leaf. Use about 1 teaspoon of salt per quarter.

❷ Spread the olive oil around in a heavy frying pan that has a lid that fits on it. Place the napa cabbage quarters in the pan with the sliced sides down, and cover with the lid. Cook over low to very low heat for 30 minutes. Check on the cabbage from time to time—once it has browned on the bottom, turn it over.

Chinese-style Steamed Napa Cabbage with Ginger, Soy and Sesame

Steam-simmered napa cabbage is served with typical Chinese seasonings—plenty of green onion and ginger, and drizzled with sizzling hot sesame oil. This makes a great main dish for special occasions or when you are entertaining.

AN EASY-TO-MAKE AMOUNT

- ½ small napa cabbage, about 1 lb 2 oz (500 g)
- ¾ cup (200 ml) water
- Pinch of salt
- 1 large green onion
- Ginger, for garnish
- 5 tablespoons sesame oil
- 5 tablespoons soy sauce
- A little ra-yu chili oil, for drizzling
- A few chili pepper threads, for garnish

① Cut the napa cabbage in half lengthwise, without removing the core. Place in a deep frying pan (or wide-bottomed pot), pour in about ¾ cup of water, add the pinch of salt, cover and steam-cook for 15–20 minutes.

② Cut the green onion into 2 inch (5 cm) long strips. Peel and shred the ginger.

③ When the napa cabbage is tender, transfer to a serving plate and top with the green onion and ginger.

④ Heat the sesame oil in a small saucepan over medium heat. When the oil is smoking hot, pour it over the napa cabbage. Pour on the soy sauce and a little chili oil, and garnish with the chili pepper threads.

⑤ When ready to eat, cut the napa cabbage into bite-size pieces, mix everything on the serving plate together and serve.

Napa Cabbage Acqua Pazza

The Italian fish dish acqua pazza is made here with vegetables only. The vegetables are poached in water rather than stock, to bring out the deep and gentle flavor of napa cabbage in season.

AN EASY-TO-MAKE AMOUNT

½ small napa cabbage, about
    1 lb 2 oz (500 g)
3–4 king oyster mushrooms
15 cherry tomatoes
2 garlic cloves, peeled and
    finely minced
2 tablespoons olive oil
1 cup (240 ml) water
10 black pitted olives
3 tablespoons shio koji
Salt, to taste
Soy sauce, to taste

❶ Cut the napa cabbage into chunks. Cut the caps of the mushrooms into wedges, and cut the stems into ½ inch (1 cm) slices. Remove the calyxes from the cherry tomatoes.
❷ In a heavy pan, sauté the garlic in the olive oil over low heat until the garlic begins to brown slightly. Add the cabbage and mushrooms and sauté over medium heat.
❸ When the napa cabbage is wilted, add 1 cup water, the cherry tomatoes, the black olives and the shio koji and cover. Bring to a boil, reduce the heat and simmer for 20 minutes.
❹ When the napa cabbage is soft and tender, season with salt and soy sauce to taste.

Napa Cabbage Salad with Ponzu Dressing

I highly recommend making this with napa cabbage when it's in season. The crispy leaves combined with grated daikon radish and sautéed mushrooms make a hearty main-dish salad.

SERVES 2

3½ oz (100 g) shimeji mushrooms
3½ oz (100 g) shiitake mushrooms
1 teaspoon sesame oil
2 tablespoons soy sauce
Leaf tips of ¼ small napa cabbage, about 9 oz (250 g)
¾ cup (165 g) grated daikon radish
Finely shredded yuzu peel, for garnish

For the Ponzu Dressing (you can also use store-bought)
3 tablespoons yuzu or lemon juice
3 tablespoons soy sauce
3 tablespoons kombu dashi stock (see page 11)
2 tablespoons ground sesame seeds
1 tablespoon ginger juice (extract by squeezing out grated ginger)

1 Cut the hard stem ends off the shimeji and divide the shimeji into small clumps. Cut the caps off the shiitake mushrooms, and thinly slice both caps and stems.
2 Heat the sesame oil in a pan over medium heat and sauté the mushrooms. When they wilt, pour 2 tablespoons soy sauce over them and turn off the heat.

3 In a bowl, mix together the ingredients for the Ponzu Dressing.
4 Tear the napa cabbage leaves into bite-size pieces, place them in a bowl, and top with the grated daikon and the sautéed mushrooms. Drizzle with the ponzu sauce and sprinkle with yuzu peel. Toss together before serving.

Stir-fried Basil with Miso

This is a miso dish that can be served as a side or as an accompaniment to rice or tofu. It's packed full of basil and the addition of almonds or pine nuts gives a wonderful texture.

AN EASY-TO-MAKE AMOUNT

4 cups (80 g) basil
1 tablespoon sesame oil
1½ oz (40 g) roughly chopped
   almonds or pine nuts
3 tablespoons miso
2 tablespoons mirin

❶ Chop the basil roughly. Heat the sesame oil in a frying pan and stir-fry the basil for 1 minute. Add the almonds or pine nuts and stir-fry further.
❷ Mix together the miso and mirin and add to the frying pan. Stir for about 1 minute while mixing well with a spatula.

Parsley and Sprouted Brown Rice Salad

Parsley is usually relegated to the role of garnish, but in this dish it's the star. Tomatoes and onions add to the color and provide a refreshing aroma. With brown rice completing the cast of main ingredients, this is a substantial salad.

1 oz (30 g) parsley
8 cherry tomatoes
3 heaping tablespoons finely minced red onion
1 cup (200 g) cooked and cooled sprouted brown rice or brown rice

A Ingredients
2 tablespoons olive oil
1 tablespoon lemon juice
1 teaspoon salt
A little allspice
A little cinnamon powder

❶ Chop the parsley finely. Remove the calyxes from the cherry tomatoes and cut into quarters.
❷ Put the A Ingredients in a large bowl and mix together. Add the red onion, mix and leave for 10 minutes.
❸ Add the rice, parsley and tomatoes to the Step 2 bowl and mix.
❹ Transfer to a container and refrigerate for at least an hour, longer if possible, to allow the flavors to blend together.

Kabayaki-style Bell Peppers

Kabayaki is a Japanese cooking method traditionally used for eel. The sweetness of the slowly fried bell peppers is enhanced by the powdered sansho pepper. These peppers are delicious when freshly cooked, but if you let them rest for a day or two before eating, they take on a real depth of flavor.

AN EASY-TO-MAKE AMOUNT

5–6 small young bell peppers, about 9 oz (250 g)
Flour, for dusting
1 tablespoon canola oil
2 tablespoons soy sauce
2 tablespoons mirin
A little sansho pepper powder, to serve

❶ Cut the bell peppers into half or quarters depending on their size, and discard the tops and seeds. Bash them flat using a pestle, a rolling pin or the side of your knife, and dust them with flour.

❷ Heat the canola oil in a frying pan, and fry the peppers slowly on both sides over medium heat. Add the soy sauce and mirin, and cook down the liquid while turning the peppers.

❸ Arrange on a serving plate and sprinkle with the sansho pepper.

Whole Bell Peppers Braised with Ginger

This is a really easy recipe where the bell peppers are cooked whole to give concentrated umami flavors. Since the seeds are eaten too, choose small peppers whose seeds are still tender.

AN EASY-TO-MAKE AMOUNT

2 teaspoons sesame oil
5–6 small young bell peppers,
**   about 9 oz (250 g)**
Small piece ginger, shredded
1 cup (240 ml) water
1½ tablespoons miso
1½ tablespoons mirin

❶ Heat the oil in a pan. Add the bell peppers and ginger and sauté over medium heat. Add the water. Cover the pan and simmer over low heat for about 10 minutes.
❷ When the bell peppers are tender, add the miso and mirin. Remove the lid and simmer over medium heat for about 5 minutes until there is almost no moisture left in the pan.

Broccoli Crumble

This versatile and flavorful broccoli topping can be served on rice, in soups or with salads. It will keep in the freezer in an airtight container for up to a month.

AN EASY-TO-MAKE AMOUNT

1 head broccoli, about 9 oz (250 g)
2 tablespoons olive oil
1 garlic clove, peeled and finely minced
1 dried red chili pepper, finely minced
½ teaspoon salt, or to taste

❶ Cut the broccoli into small pieces and process in a food processor or chop with a knife into very fine pieces.
❷ Put the 2 tablespoons of olive oil and the garlic in a frying pan and sauté over low heat until the garlic is slightly colored. Add the broccoli and the chili pepper and sauté over medium heat to combine. When the mixture is moist and brightly colored, season with ½ teaspoon salt or to taste.

Using the Broccoli Crumble

Broccoli Crumble Spaghetti

Broccoli Crumble can be made into a first-rate pasta sauce by simply adding olive oil and pasta cooking water. This dish is hearty and very satisfying.

SERVES 2

Salt, to taste
7 oz (200 g) spaghetti
Olive oil, for stir-frying
Broccoli Crumble from the above recipe, the whole amount

❶ Bring a pot of salted water to a boil, and cook the spaghetti for 1 minute less than indicated on the package. Drain the spaghetti and reserve the cooking water.
❷ Heat the olive oil in a frying pan over medium heat. Add the Broccoli Crumble and about 2 ladles of the spaghetti cooking water. Add the spaghetti to the pan, stir-fry for about 1 minute and season with a pinch of salt.

Broccoli Burgers with Miso Sauce

These colorful mini-burgers are made using the Broccoli Crumble mixture as a base, and pan-frying. The spicy tomato sauce, enriched with miso, is the perfect complement.

SERVES 2

Broccoli Crumble from recipe on facing page, the whole amount
Olive oil, for frying

A Ingredients
6½ tablespoons panko bread-crumbs
3½ tablespoons grated Chinese yam
3 tablespoons flour

For the Sauce
Tomato purée, to taste
Miso, to taste
Hot pepper sauce, to taste

❶ Put the Broccoli Crumble and the A Ingredients in a bowl and mix together well with your hands. Divide into 8 portions and form into patties.
❷ Combine the sauce ingredients in a small bowl, adjusting the quantities of each ingredient to your taste.
❸ Heat a little olive oil in a frying pan and put in the patties. Cook them slowly over low heat. When both sides are browned, transfer to a serving plate and top with the sauce.

Broccoli Pakoras

These Indian-style fritters have a thin batter that is full of tasty spices.
They are fried until the outside is crispy and the inside is soft and tender.

AN EASY-TO-MAKE AMOUNT

1 head broccoli, about 9 oz
   (250 g)
Oil, for frying
Lemon wedges, to serve
Salt, to serve

For the Batter
¾ cup (200 ml) cold water
Scant 1 cup (100 g) flour
½ tablespoon ginger juice
   (extract by squeezing out
   grated ginger)
½ tablespoon coriander powder
½ tablespoon cumin powder
Scant 1 teaspoon salt
A little chili powder

1 Cut the broccoli into small florets. Mix the batter ingredients briefly.
2 Put oil in a frying pan to a depth of ¾ inch (2 cm). Turn the heat to medium. When the oil is hot, add the broccoli. Cook, turning, until golden brown.
3 Transfer to a serving plate and serve with lemon wedges and salt on the side.

> **NOTE** Making the most of broccoli
>
> Broccoli is often eaten boiled, but since it is compatible with oil and easily cooked through, I recommend deep-frying or stir-frying it. Cooking it in oil has the advantage of giving it more depth of flavor. Broccoli does not have a strong flavor of its own, so if you are making tempura or otherwise deep-frying it, add spices to the batter. Cumin, coriander, chili, ginger, and garlic—or just curry powder—are recommended.

Jellied Spinach and Mushrooms

The smooth refreshing texture of this dish goes well with both rice and sake. You can use a clear glass to mold the jelly, making a visually stunning dish that will impress your guests.

AN EASY-TO-MAKE AMOUNT

7 oz (200 g) spinach
3½ oz (100 g) enoki mushrooms
3½ oz (100 g) nameko mushrooms
3 shiitake mushrooms
Grated ginger, for garnish
Soy sauce, to serve

A Ingredients
2 cups (480 ml) kombu dashi stock (see page 11)
1 teaspoon agar-agar powder
Scant 1 teaspoon salt
Dash of soy sauce

❶ Remove the root ends of the spinach, and boil the spinach briefly. Drain, squeeze out the water and cut into ½ inch (1.5 cm) lengths. Cut off the root ends of the enoki and nameko and cut the mushrooms into ½ inch (1.5 cm) lengths. Discard the stems of the shiitake mushrooms, cut the caps in half and slice the caps thinly.

❷ Stir the A Ingredients in a pan over medium heat, bring to a boil, and add the spinach and mushrooms. When the pan comes to a boil again, remove from the heat, pour the mixture into a mold that has been wet with water and refrigerate until the mixture has set.

❸ Cut the jelly into bite-size pieces, place in a bowl and top with some grated ginger. Serve with some soy sauce on the side for dipping.

Hot and Sour Spinach Soup

The umami provided by the shiitake mushrooms means that no stock is needed. Spinach and mushrooms are a particularly delicious combination.

AN EASY-TO-MAKE AMOUNT

7 oz (200 g) spinach
5 dried shiitake mushrooms, soaked and reconstituted (reserve the soaking water)
½ tablespoon sesame oil
1 dried red chili pepper, finely minced
2 tablespoons kudzu powder

A Ingredients

½ large green onion, finely minced
Small piece ginger, finely minced
¼ onion, finely minced

B Ingredients

4 tablespoons rice vinegar
3 tablespoons soy sauce
Scant 1 teaspoon salt
A little black pepper

❶ Boil the spinach, drain and put into cold water. Drain again and squeeze out, and cut into 1 inch (2.5 inch) pieces. Remove the stems from the shiitake and discard. Slice the caps thinly.
❷ Put the sesame oil and the A Ingredients in a pan and sauté slowly over medium-low heat. Add the shiitake mushrooms and red chili pepper and sauté some more. Add 5 cups (1.2 L) of the water used to soak the shiitake (adding extra water if needed to make 5 cups) and raise the heat to medium. When the pan comes to a boil turn the heat to low, simmer for 2 minutes then add the B Ingredients.

❸ Add the spinach and bring back to a boil. Dissolve the kudzu powder in 2 tablespoons of water and add to the soup to thicken it.

Indian-style Mizuna Greens

Mizuna greens, a classic ingredient in Japanese-style hot pots, are the stars of the show here. Two whole bunches of mizuna greens are used in this nutrient-packed dish. You can make this with komatsuna greens or cabbage too.

AN EASY-TO-MAKE AMOUNT

2 bunches mizuna greens, about 14 oz (400 g) total
1 tablespoon canola oil
2 teaspoons cumin seeds
1 garlic clove, peeled and finely minced
Small piece ginger, finely minced
Scant ½ teaspoon turmeric powder, or 1 teaspoon curry powder
1 teaspoon salt

❶ Cut the mizuna greens into 1 inch (2.5 cm) long pieces. Heat the canola oil and cumin seeds in a frying pan over low heat. When small bubbles form around the cumin seeds, add the garlic and ginger and sauté until fragrant.
❷ Increase the heat, add the mizuna greens and sauté until wilted. Season with the turmeric powder and salt.

Spanish-style Radishes in Garlic

Twenty whole radishes are used in this dish. The cooking process makes them sweet and irresistible. Let them rest a little before eating so the flavors blend.

AN EASY-TO-MAKE AMOUNT

20 radishes, about 7 oz (200 g) total
1 garlic clove
6½ tablespoons olive oil
1 teaspoon salt, or to taste
1 teaspoon lemon juice
Pinch of red chili pepper flakes

❶ Cut the leaves off the radishes and discard. Cut each radish into half lengthwise. Peel the garlic clove and smash flat with the side of a knife.

❷ Place all the ingredients in a pan and cook over low heat until the radishes are tender. Leave to cool so the flavors can blend together, and reheat when ready to serve.

Leaf Lettuce Stir-fried with Garlic

This recipe uses two whole heads of lettuce for a hearty and healthy dish.
The crunchy texture which is unique to this lettuce stir-fry is addictive.

AN EASY-TO-MAKE AMOUNT

2 heads leaf lettuce, about
   1 lb 2 oz (500 g) total
2 garlic cloves, peeled and
   finely minced
3 tablespoons olive oil
Salt, for seasoning
1 dried red chili pepper, finely
   minced
1 teaspoon soy sauce, or to
   taste

❶ Tear the lettuce into large
pieces.
❷ In a large frying pan over low
heat, sauté the garlic in the olive
oil until slightly browned, then
increase the heat. Add the leaf
lettuce in about 5 batches as you
stir-fry. Sprinkle in a pinch of
salt with each addition, and stir-
fry slowly until wilted.
❸ When the lettuce is reduced
in bulk by about one fifth, add
the red chili pepper and stir-fry
some more. Taste and adjust
with a little more salt and the
soy sauce.

NOTE

Making the most of lettuce

Lettuce can be cooked or pickled to reduce its bulk. In this recipe, two heads of leaf lettuce are slowly
stir-fried. Although the crispy texture is retained, the bulk is reduced to about one fifth of the original,
so you can eat a lot of lettuce. As well as stir-frying it, as in this recipe, lettuce lends itself well to simmering. Lettuce is also great as a pickle: see my recipe for Lightly Pickled Iceberg Lettuce on page 103.

PICKLING:
Preserved Goodness

The Appeal of Pickling

Pickling is wisdom passed down by our ancestors to preserve food for extended periods of time. There are several ways to preserve food: by removing water from the ingredients with salt or sugar; by pickling in fermented foods such as soy sauce or miso; or by lacto-fermentation of the ingredients themselves. Lacto-fermentation refers to the decomposition and fermentation of carbohydrates in vegetables by the lactic acid bacteria attached to the vegetables.

The best thing about preserved food is the way its taste changes. If you pickle the same type of vegetable on different occasions, the results will always vary in taste. I find that seasonal vegetables—which have a certain strength to them—always make good pickles.

The interesting aspect of the pickling process is that you cannot control the bacteria. Fermented foods are influenced by the health and mood of the person making them, so ones that are made when I'm not feeling well are often not so good. I hope you will have fun experimenting with the pickling recipes in this section of the book when you are in good physical condition.

How to Preserve and Store Food Well

Pickle at room temperature, then refrigerate

For vegetables that are preserved using lacto-fermentation methods, it is especially important to activate the lactic acid bacteria at the beginning of pickling, to prevent the growth of unwanted bacteria. Since a warm environment is better for fermentation, vegetables should be kept at room temperature prior to pickling, and then stored in the refrigerator after fermentation.

Each recipe in this section gives the shelf life for every pickle, but it is only a guide. If pickles are stored well, they may keep for a longer period of time.

Keep to the amount of salt specified

You may be tempted to reduce the amount of salt called for in these pickling recipes because of concerns about consuming too much sodium. However, reducing the amount of salt when pickling increases the likelihood of spoilage. This is because most spoilage bacteria are inhibited by salt. In the case of lacto-fermentation, lactobacilli are salt-tolerant, so there is no need to worry.

Use fresh, washed vegetables

Not-so-fresh vegetables may spoil when pickled, so use fresh ones. Vegetables contain lactic acid bacteria necessary for lacto-fermentation but the soil in which they are grown may contain unwanted bacteria that can cause spoilage. Before pickling, vegetables should be washed just enough to remove the soil. Make sure to drain off the excess water after washing, so that the salt content in the pickling liquid does not become too diluted, as this can also lead to spoilage.

Keep containers, utensils, and the refrigerator clean

Disinfect all equipment used in the pickling process with boiling water or food-grade alcohol to prevent the growth of bacteria. This applies not just to the containers and weights used during the fermentation process but to the equipment used to prepare the vegetables such as knives and colanders.. In addition to keeping the refrigerator clean, use sterilized utensils (forks, spoons, chopsticks, etc) when removing pickles from the containers in which they are stored.

Use airtight containers

Tightly sealed containers and bags are effective in keeping food free of unwanted bacteria. Lactic acid bacteria are particularly sensitive to oxygen, so a well-sealed container is crucial to successful pickling.

Different types of pickling suit different types of container. When pickling vegetables in a pickling solution, a bag is a good way to distribute the seasoning throughout the vegetables. When vegetables are soaked in brine for lacto-fermentation, storage jars or containers are recommended due to the large amount of juice. For longer storage (more than one month), use double-layered heavy duty plastic bags.

For other pickling methods, you can use jars, containers or bags.

How to Enjoy Pickled Vegetables

Once you're in the swing of making your own pickles, you'll find so many ways to use them. Here are some of my favorites.

Use pickles instead of seasonings

Since pickles are salty, they are best paired with light tasting foods. They are delicious served on hot rice or steamed potatoes, with tofu, or mixed into a dressing or purée.

Use as an additional ingredient

I also recommend using pickles in fried rice and as dumpling filling. Lacto-fermented vegetables such as kimchi or traditional Japanese shibazuke pickles (see page 98) have a particularly strong umami that goes beyond simple saltiness for a real depth of flavor.

Use as a stock

The juice from pickles should not be discarded. It can be used as a base for soups and hot pots, or added to sauces.

If the acidity of the vegetables has increased over time after pickling, they become easier to eat when heated. If the vegetables themselves are lacto-fermented, heating will kill the lactobacilli, but the lactobacilli will still feed the good bacteria in the intestines, so plenty of health benefits can be expected.

Tomatoes in Syrup with Ginger

Large in-season tomatoes are fermented with fresh ginger and maple syrup. This is refreshing when the weather is hot.

AN EASY-TO-MAKE AMOUNT

5 large tomatoes, about 2 lb 4 oz (1 kg) total
Piece tender new ginger, about 3½ oz (100 g)
¾ cup (200 ml) maple syrup

1 Remove the calyxes and cut each tomato into 8–12 wedges. Thinly slice the ginger with the skin on.
2 Combine the tomatoes, ginger and maple syrup in a thick plastic bag and seal tightly. Store in the refrigerator. This can be eaten from the next day. It will continue to ferment as it is stored and the bag will puff up, so open the bag and release the air periodically.

> ***SHELF LIFE:** 1 week in the refrigerator*

Using the Tomatoes in Syrup with Ginger

Tomatoes in Syrup with Ginger and Soda

The richly flavored syrup produced by fermenting the tomatoes makes a delicious drink.

AN EASY-TO-MAKE AMOUNT

Pour equal parts of the syrup from the tomatoes, and soda water into a glass. Add some of the pickled tomatoes and ginger.

Fermented Tomato Sauce

Tomatoes are fermented with sugar and salt in this sauce, which is not cooked. Just a small amount added to a dish will give it an extra dimension of deliciousness.

AN EASY-TO-MAKE AMOUNT

**5 large tomatoes, about
   2 lb 4 oz (1 kg)**
1 dried red chili pepper

A Ingredients
**2 tablespoons raw cane sugar
   or beet sugar**
2 tablespoons salt
2 teaspoons grated garlic clove

❶ Remove the calyxes and cut each tomato into 4 wedges. Put into a blender or food processor with the A Ingredients and blend. Pour into a thick plastic bag, add the chili pepper and seal tightly.
❷ Ferment at room temperature for 1 day, then refrigerate for 1 further day. It is then ready to eat.

> ***SHELF LIFE: 2 weeks in the refrigerator**

Summer Vegetable Curry with Fermented Tomato Sauce

The addition of fermented tomato sauce gives the curry a richness and umami—as if it had been simmered for a long time. Here I've used eggplant and kabocha squash, but you can use any vegetables you like.

AN EASY-TO-MAKE AMOUNT

1 slender Asian eggplant, about 3 oz (80 g)
3½ oz (100 g) kabocha squash
1 tablespoon canola oil
2 teaspoons curry powder
6½ tablespoons Fermented Tomato Sauce (see facing page)
Salt, to taste
Cooked rice, to serve

❶ Remove the top from the eggplant and cut into rough pieces. Remove the seeds and pith from the kabocha squash and cut into rough pieces, leaving the skin on.

❷ Heat the canola oil in a frying pan over medium heat, and sauté the eggplant and kabocha pieces.

❸ Add the curry powder and sauté until fragrant. Add the Fermented Tomato Sauce, cover the pan and simmer over low heat. When the vegetables are soft, add salt to taste.

❹ Serve with rice.

Cherry Tomatoes Pickled in Miso

Peel the skins of the cherry tomatoes before putting them in the miso bed so that they soak up more goodness. The umami of the tomatoes and of the miso combine to create a deep flavor.

AN EASY-TO-MAKE AMOUNT

12–13 cherry tomatoes, about 7 oz
   (200 g)
3 tablespoons barley miso, or mild
   miso of your choice
Pinch of red chili pepper powder

❶ Remove the calyxes from the cherry tomatoes. Dunk them for a few seconds in boiling water, and peel off the skins.
❷ Put the peeled tomatoes, miso and chili pepper in a plastic bag, and leave to marinate for at least 1 hour.

*SHELF LIFE: 1–2 days in the refrigerator

Cucumber Narazuke Pickles

Narazuke is a traditional type of pickle originating from Nara in Japan. It uses sake lees, a by-product of the sake-making process. If possible, use sake lees that have been well aged. Try inquiring at a sake brewery if there's one near you.

AN EASY-TO-MAKE AMOUNT

**10 small Asian cucumbers,
    about 2 lbs 4 oz (1 kg) total
2⅔ tablespoons salt
11 lbs (5 kg) sake lees**

❶ Prepare the cucumbers. Sprinkle them with the salt, put them in one layer in a shallow container, and cover the surface tightly with plastic wrap. Put a 2–4½ lb (1–2 kg) weight on top, and leave until water comes out of the cucumbers and they are completely immersed in that water.

❷ Drain off the water from the cucumbers, put them on a flat sieve or colander and dry in the sun for half a day. (If it is cloudy or rainy, place the cucumbers in a food dehydrator or in a switched off oven with the door slightly ajar for a few hours until they have shriveled a little.)

❸ Fill a large, heavy-duty plastic bag with the sake lees. Add the cucumbers, eliminate all the air in the bag and leave to pickle in a cool, dark place for 1 year.

***SHELF LIFE:** More than 2 years in a cool, dark place or the vegetable compartment of the refrigerator*

TIP: After one year of pickling you can put the cucumbers into a fresh batch of 11 lb (5 kg) of sake lees and leave for another year. More salt will leech out and they will become even more mellow and tasty.

Lacto-fermented Cucumber Pickles

This non-sour cucumber pickle is lacto-fermented. Enjoy the lactobacillus-rich pickling juice too—try it as a base for soups, sauces or hot pots.

**12 small Asian cucumbers,
  about 2½ lbs (1.2 kg) total**
5 cups (1.2 L) water
3 tablespoons salt
2 dried red chili peppers
10 whole black peppercorns
2 cloves
1–2 bay leaves

❶ Cut the cucumbers in half lengthwise (or quarter them if they are large).
❷ Put all the ingredients except the cucumbers into a preserving jar or container and stir to dissolve the salt. Immerse the cucumbers completely in the liquid, and leave to ferment for half to a full day if it is summer and the room temperature is warm. (If the room temperature is cooler, leave to ferment for up to twice as long.) When small bubbles form and you can taste a mild sourness and umami from the pickling liquid, the pickles are ready to eat.

*SHELF LIFE: 2 weeks in the refrigerator

Creamy Yogurt Soup with Cucumber Pickles

The pickling juice from the Lacto-fermented Cucumber Pickles goes really well with the mild flavor of unsweetened soy yogurt.

SERVES 2

6½ tablespoons pickling liquid from the Lacto-fermented Cucumber Pickles (see facing page)
1 cup (240 g) unsweetened soy yogurt
1 tablespoon olive oil
Salt, to taste
A few slices of Lacto-fermented Cucumber Pickles

❶ Combine all the ingredients except the slices of cucumber pickle.
❷ Serve topped with thin slices of cucumber pickle.

Vegan Cucumber Kimchi

This lightly pickled kimchi makes the most of the fresh taste of the cucumbers and will keep you coming back for more.

AN EASY-TO-MAKE AMOUNT

10 small Asian cucumbers, about 2 lb 4 oz (1 kg) total
2 tablespoons salt

A Ingredients
4 tablespoons coarsely ground red chili pepper
2 tablespoons roasted sesame seeds
1 tablespoon grated ginger
3 tablespoons shio koji
½ grated Asian pear

❶ Cut the cucumbers roughly into long thin pieces. Sprinkle with the salt.

❷ Layer the cucumbers in a shallow container and place plastic wrap directly on top of them. Put a 2–4½ lb (1–2 kg) weight on top of the plastic wrap, and leave until water comes out of the cucumbers and they are completely immersed in that water. Leave the immersed cucumbers for half to a full day if it is summer at room temperature to ferment. (If the room temperature is cooler, leave for twice as long.) Drain the cucumbers in a colander without pressing down on them.

❸ Mix the A Ingredients in a large bowl. Add the cucumbers and mix. Put into a jar, container or heavy-duty plastic bag and refrigerate. They are best eaten after 3 days to 1 week.

*SHELF LIFE: Finish eating them after refrigerating them within a week to 10 days. This does not keep for a long time.

Stir-fried Vegan Cucumber Kimchi with Tofu

Adding the pickling liquid as well as the cucumbers from the
Vegan Cucumber Kimchi gives a rich and satisfying flavor.

SERVES 2

**1 block atsuage thick fried tofu,
about 9 oz (250 g)**
1 tablespoon sesame oil
**1 large or 2 small cucumbers
worth of cucumbers from
Vegan Cucumber Kimchi (see
facing page)**
**2 tablespoons pickling liquid
from Vegan Cucumber
Kimchi**
Salt and pepper, to taste

❶ Using your hands, break the
tofu into bite-size pieces.
❷ Heat the sesame oil in a frying pan over medium heat. Add
the cucumbers and fried tofu
and stir-fry.
❸ Add the pickling liquid and
continue stir-frying. Adjust the
taste with salt and pepper.

Eggplant Shibazuke Pickles

Shibazuke is a traditional pickle that originates from Kyoto.
The lacto-fermentation process for shibazuke can only be
done during the warmer months of the year.

AN EASY-TO-MAKE AMOUNT

6 slender Asian eggplants, about 1 lb 2 oz (500 g) total
5½ oz (150 g) red shiso leaves
2 tablespoons salt (1% of the weight of the eggplants)

1 Remove and discard the tops of the eggplants, and cut each eggplant into ¼ inch (5 mm) thick diagonal slices. Wash the red shiso leaves well and dry them.

2 In a container or double-layered plastic bag, layer the ingredients in this order: salt, eggplant, salt, shiso leaves. Continue the layering until all the ingredients have been used, finishing with a layer of shiso. Press down firmly with your hands. Sprinkle salt on the final layer.

3 If using a jar or container, cover the surface tightly with plastic wrap, place a 1 lb 2 oz (500 g) weight on top and cover with a lid. If pickling in a plastic bag, remove air from the bag and close the bag tightly. Leave overnight.

4 Next day, when plenty of water has come out of the eggplants, move them to a well-ventilated place out of direct sunlight and leave to ferment for 2 weeks in summer (or longer at cooler times of the year). When fermented, store the eggplants in the pickling liquid in the refrigerator. If you are storing in a plastic bag, check regularly for leaks.

Eggplant Pickled in Amazake

Fermented in amazake (sweet sake, see page 9), these pickles are mild, sweet and salty all at once—I find it really hard to stop eating them once I've started!

AN EASY-TO-MAKE AMOUNT

10 slender Asian eggplants, about 1 lb 12 oz (800 g) total
2½ tablespoons salt (5% of the weight of the eggplants)

For the Pickling Bed
4 cups (1 L) thick amazake (see page 9 for recipe)
3½ oz (100 g) mustard powder, or to taste

❶ Make the pickling bed. Mix the ingredients together, put into a preserving container, and cover tightly with plastic wrap. Cover the container with a lid and refrigerate for 2 days.

❷ Prepare the eggplants. Remove and discard the tops of the eggplants and slice each eggplant into quarters lengthwise. Sprinkle with salt, but do not rub in. Layer the eggplant pieces in a shallow container and cover tightly with plastic wrap. Place a weight on top twice as heavy as the eggplants and leave at room temperature overnight, so that the water in the eggplants will come out.

❸ Pickle the eggplants. Squeeze the moisture firmly out of the eggplant pieces. Spread the Step 1 mixture on each piece as you pack them into a preserving jar, container or large thick plastic bag. If using a jar or container put on the lid. If using a bag, eliminate the air and close it up tightly. Put in the refrigerator. They are ready to eat in about 4 days.

*SHELF LIFE: 2 weeks in the refrigerator

Thinly Sliced Pickled Eggplant

Thinly sliced eggplant is lacto-fermented with salt and water. The gentle sourness and saltiness of this pickle are exquisite, and it can be served with rice or as a snack with drinks.

AN EASY-TO-MAKE AMOUNT

10 slender Asian eggplants, about 1 lb 12 oz (800 g) total
2 tablespoons salt
4 cups (1 L) water

❶ Remove and discard the tops of the eggplants and cut each eggplant into ¼ inch (5 mm) thick diagonal slices. Mix the salt and water to make a brine.

❷ Put the eggplant slices in a preserving jar or container, and pour in the brine. Place a light weight, such as plate, on top of the eggplants so that they are completely immersed in the brine. Cover the container tightly with plastic wrap.

❸ Keep covered at room temperature for 1–2 days in summer (twice as long if the weather is cooler), then store in a refrigerator after lacto-fermentation occurs. When the brine turns slightly purple with small bubbles and has a soft acidity and umami, the lacto-fermentation has been completed.

> ***SHELF LIFE: 2 weeks in the refrigerator**

Using the Thinly Sliced Pickled Eggplant

Pickled Eggplant Hors d'Oeuvre

Just add dill and olive oil to make a great starter or snack. Basil or chives also work well in place of dill.

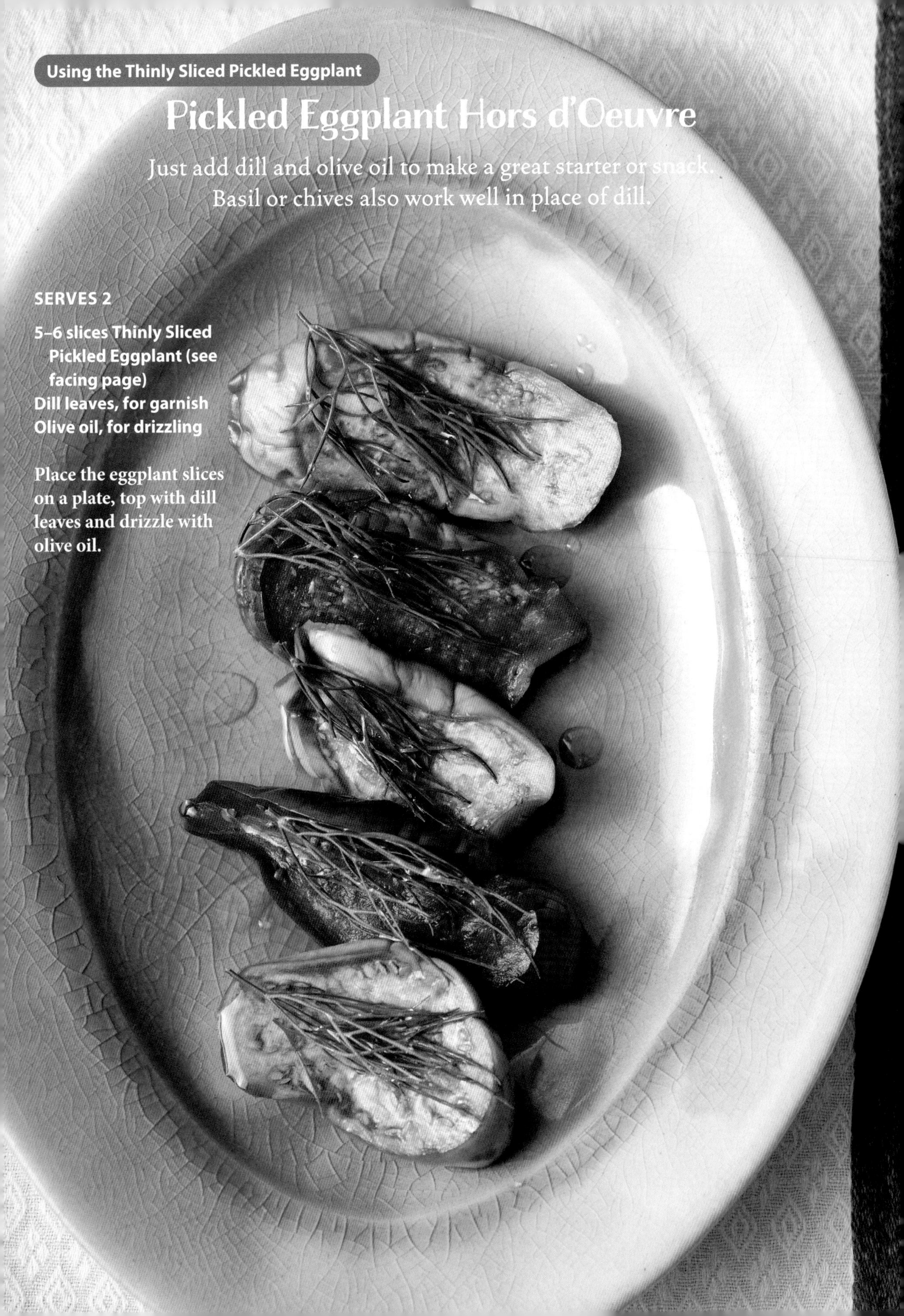

SERVES 2

5–6 slices Thinly Sliced Pickled Eggplant (see facing page)
Dill leaves, for garnish
Olive oil, for drizzling

Place the eggplant slices on a plate, top with dill leaves and drizzle with olive oil.

Pickled Bell Peppers and Shiso

Bell peppers are first lacto-fermented, and then marinated in soy sauce. They become tender and delicious, and their strong flavor is softened.

AN EASY-TO-MAKE AMOUNT

15 small young green bell peppers, about
   1 lb 2 oz (500 g) total
1¼ tablespoons salt
4 cups (1 L) water
30 green shiso leaves
⅔ cup (150 ml) soy sauce

❶ Halve the bell peppers. Remove and discard the tops and seeds. Put the salt and water in a preserving jar or container, stir to dissolve the salt, then add the bell peppers. Leave the bell peppers completely immersed in the salt water for half to a full day in summer (longer in cooler weather) to lacto-ferment them. Drain into a colander without squeezing.

❷ Place the peppers and shiso leaves in a jar, container, or heavy-duty plastic bag and pour in the soy sauce. If using a jar or container, place plastic wrap directly on top of the contents and place a 1 lb 2 oz (500 g) weight on top of the plastic wrap to keep the peppers covered with soy sauce. If using a bag, remove all the air, close the mouth, and place a 1 lb 2 oz weight on top. Store in the refrigerator. The peppers are ready to eat the next day.

*SHELF LIFE: 2 weeks in the refrigerator

Using the Pickled Bell Peppers and Shiso

Tofu with Pickled Bell Peppers and Shiso

The salty taste of soy sauce makes this pickle a great addition to any dish.

Mince the Pickled Bell Peppers and Shiso finely and serve as a garnish for cold tofu.

Lightly Pickled Iceberg Lettuce

The lettuce is pickled in salt with a weight on it to remove the water
and reduce its bulk, so you can eat one whole head in no time,
while still enjoying its crispy texture.

AN EASY-TO-MAKE AMOUNT

**1 large head iceberg lettuce, about 10–14 oz
 (300–400 g)**
**2 pieces kombu seaweed, each 1 inch (2.5 cm)
 square**

A Ingredients
¾ cup (200 ml) water
1 tablespoon salt
1 dried red chili pepper

1 Tear the iceberg lettuce into quarters with
your hands. Shred the kombu seaweed finely
using scissors.
2 Place the lettuce and kombu seaweed and the
A Ingredients in a bowl or container. Place a piece
of plastic wrap directly on top of the lettuce, and
put a 2 lb 4 oz (1 kg) weight on top of the plastic
wrap. The lettuce is ready to eat after leaving to
pickle overnight.

*SHELF LIFE: 1 week in the refrigerator

Vegan Napa Cabbage Kimchi

No garlic is used in this vegan kimchi so it has a mild taste.
As it develops sourness over time it can be used
in stir-fries, stews and other dishes.

AN EASY-TO-MAKE AMOUNT

Large head napa cabbage, about 4½ lbs(2 kg)

5 tablespoons salt (4% of the weight of the napa cabbage)

For the Kimchi Pickling Base

14 oz (400 g) daikon radish, peeled

1 oz (30 g) garlic chives

½ onion

14 oz (400 g) leeks or large green onions

1 tablespoon roasted sesame seeds

2 tablespoons shio koji

¾ cup (200 ml) water

Piece kombu seaweed, about 4 inches x 1 inch (10 cm x 2.5 cm)

1 tablespoon glutinous rice flour (mochiko) or regular rice flour

A Ingredients

⅔ cup (60 g) chili powder or flakes (Korean preferred)

1 tablespoon grated ginger

1 Asian pear, grated

2 tablespoons shio koji

> *SHELF LIFE: 1 month in a cool dark place or the refrigerator

❶ Strip off the rough outer leaves of the cabbage and reserve. Cut a lengthwise slit into the cabbage from the base of the head to the center. Insert your thumb into the slit and rip into four equal pieces. Cut off the base. Sprinkle the salt on both sides of each leaf and let stand overnight. Rinse in cold water, place in a colander with the root end up and the top down. Let drain for 1–2 hours.

❷ For the Kimchi Picking Base, cut the radish into 1½ inch (4 cm) lengths. Chop the garlic chives. Slice the onion thinly lengthwise. Halve the leeks then cut into thin diagonal slices. Grind the sesame seeds roughly.

❸ Put the radish from Step 2 into a bowl and sprinkle with the 2 tablespoons of shio koji. When the shio koji has been absorbed, add the other Step 2 ingredients to the bowl with the radish and mix together.

❹ Make a dashi stock by putting the ¾ cup of water and the kombu in a pot and heating until the water is about to come to a boil. Remove from the heat and leave to cool. Take out the kombu and cut into thin strips. Add the rice flour to the cooled dashi stock, stir to dissolve, and place over low-medium heat. Bring to a boil, and when the mixture has thickened, allow it to cool.

❺ Combine the A Ingredients, and add the Step 3 and Step 4 ingredients to complete the Kimchi Pickling Base.

❻ Spread the Kimchi Pickling Base between the leaves of the napa cabbage, and wrap the whole cabbage with the reserved outer leaves. Put into a tightly sealed container without leaving any gaps between the leaves, cover the leaves with plastic wrap and close the lid. Leave to ferment in a cool dry place for 4 days, and it is ready to eat.

Nepalese Daikon Pickles

This is a recipe I learned when I spent two years in Nepal. The use of both white sesame seeds and sesame oil gives the dish a rich flavor.

AN EASY-TO-MAKE AMOUNT

**1 large daikon radish, about
 2 lb 4 oz (1 kg)**
**½ cup (120 g) ground white sesame
 seeds**
**5 green chili peppers, or to taste,
 sliced into rounds**
2 tablespoons salt
½ cup (120 ml) sesame oil
1 tablespoon cumin seeds

> ***SHELF LIFE: 2 weeks in the
> refrigerator**

1 Wash the daikon well, cut into quarters lengthwise, and then into ½ inch (1 cm) thick slices. Place the slices on a flat sieve or colander and dry in the sun for 1–2 days. (If it is cloudy or rainy, place them in a food dehydrator or in a switched off oven with the door slightly ajar for a few hours until they have shriveled a bit.)

2 Put the dried daikon in a heatproof bowl, sprinkle with the ground sesame seeds, add the green chili peppers and the 2 tablespoons salt and mix.

3 Heat the sesame oil and cumin seeds in a frying pan over low heat. When it starts to bubble and become fragrant, take off the heat, pour into the Step 2 bowl and mix. It is ready to eat after leaving in the fridge for half a day for the flavors to blend.

Cabbage and Water Kimchi

Cabbage, which is said to regulate gastrointestinal functions, is lacto-fermented to make it more delicious as well as increase its health benefits. Be sure to eat it with the pickling liquid to give a boost to your digestive system.

AN EASY-TO-MAKE AMOUNT

½ small cabbage, about 14 oz (400 g)
1 apple
10 green onions
Small piece ginger, shredded
2 garlic cloves, peeled and thinly sliced
1 teaspoon salt

A Ingredients

3¼ cups (800 ml) water
1 tablespoon maple syrup
2 teaspoons rice flour
2 teaspoons salt

❶ Cut the cabbage roughly. Quarter and core the apple, and slice thinly with the peel on. Cut the green onions into 1 inch (2.5 inch) long pieces.
❷ Put the Step 1 ingredients and the ginger and garlic in a bowl, sprinkle with the 1 teaspoon of salt and rub it in. Leave for a while until the vegetables are wilted, and drain off any water that came out, without squeezing the vegetables.
❸ Combine the A Ingredients in a pan and bring to a boil over medium heat. Remove from the heat and leave to cool. Transfer to a storage container, add the Step 2 ingredients, cover and leave to ferment for 1–2 days at room temperature. Serve with the liquid.

*SHELF LIFE: 1 week in the refrigerator

Salted Rakkyo-style Leeks

Salted rakkyo are a type of traditional Japanese onion pickle. This pickle, made with leeks or large green onions, has a fragrance and sourness from the first bite, followed by a spiciness and a depth of flavor.

AN EASY-TO-MAKE AMOUNT

4 leeks or fat green onions, about 11 oz (320 g) total
Salt, for sprinkling

A Ingredients
½ tablespoon salt (2.5% of the weight of the leeks)
2 teaspoons apple cider vinegar or rice vinegar
1 dried red chili pepper

❶ Cut the leeks or green onions into 1 inch (2.5 cm) lengths, place in a bowl, sprinkle with a little salt, and lightly toss. Let stand for 30 minutes, then rinse to remove any pungency and drain well.
❷ Transfer to a bowl, add the A Ingredients and mix together. Place a plate directly on top of the leeks, and a 2 lb 4 oz (1 kg) weight on the plate. Leave overnight, until the water comes out of the leeks.

*SHELF LIFE: 1 week in the refrigerator

Index of Recipes by Main Ingredient

Published by Tuttle Publishing, an imprint of
Periplus Editions (HK) Ltd.

www.tuttlepublishing.com

YASAI NO CHIKARA WO HIKIDASU!
KANO YUMIKO NO KONO YASAI DE
DODON TO IPPIN RECIPE
© Kano Yumiko 2022
English translation rights arranged with NHK
Publishing, Inc. through Japan UNI Agency, Inc.,
Tokyo

English translation by Makiko Itoh. English translation
copyright © 2024 Periplus Editions (HK) Ltd.
Photographs page 9, 11–15 all Shutterstock.com

ISBN: 978-4-8053-1745-7

27 26 25 24   5 4 3 2 1
Printed in China   2401EP

TUTTLE PUBLISHING® is a registered trademark of Tuttle Publishing, a division of
Periplus Editions (HK) Ltd.

DISTRIBUTED BY

North America, Latin America & Europe
Tuttle Publishing
364 Innovation Drive
North Clarendon, VT 05759-9436 U.S.A.
Tel: 1 (802) 773-8930; Fax: 1 (802) 773-6993
info@tuttlepublishing.com
www.tuttlepublishing.com

Japan
Tuttle Publishing
Yaekari Building 3rd Floor
5-4-12 Osaki, Shinagawa-ku
Tokyo 141-0032
Tel: (81) 3 5437-0171; Fax: (81) 3 5437-0755
sales@tuttle.co.jp
www.tuttle.co.jp

Asia Pacific
Berkeley Books Pte. Ltd.
3 Kallang Sector #04-01
Singapore 349278
Tel: (65) 6741 2178; Fax: (65) 6741 2179
inquiries@periplus.com.sg
www.tuttlepublishing.com

"Books to Span the East and West"

Tuttle Publishing was founded in 1832 in the small New England town of Rutland, Vermont [USA]. Our core values remain as strong today as they were then—to publish best-in-class books which bring people together one page at a time. In 1948, we established a publishing outpost in Japan—and Tuttle is now a leader in publishing English-language books about the arts, languages and cultures of Asia. The world has become a much smaller place today and Asia's economic and cultural influence has grown. Yet the need for meaningful dialogue and information about this diverse region has never been greater. Over the past seven decades, Tuttle has published thousands of books on subjects ranging from martial arts and paper crafts to language learning and literature—and our talented authors, illustrators, designers and photographers have won many prestigious awards. We welcome you to explore the wealth of information available on Asia at **www.tuttlepublishing.com**.